SHOCK TACTICS

A FLASH FROM THE FUTURE

SHOCK TACTICS

A FLASH FROM THE FUTURE

PETER GRAYSTONE • PAUL SHARPE • PIPPA TURNER

Scripture Union

207-209 Queensway • Bletchley • Milton Keynes • Bucks • MK2 2EB

Scripture Union, 207–209 Queensway, Bletchley,
MK2 2EB, England.

First published 1996

ISBN 0 86201 948 6

British Library Cataloguing-in-Publication Data
A catalogue record for this book is available
from the British Library.

Cover design by Ross Advertising & Design
Limited.

Design and illustration by Blue Pig Design Co.

Printed and bound in Great Britain by Ebenezer Baylis & Son Limited, The Trinity Press, Worcester and London.

Contents

AND THERE'S MORE!

SHOCKTACTICS: a flash from the future has a twin volume – **SHOCKTACTICS:** a blast from the past – which is available where you bought this book. It focuses on the claims of Jesus and their relevance. The questions it deals with are:

1. Who is Jesus?
2. Admire Jesus, yes – but why worship him?
3. Did Jesus rise from the dead?
4. Can Jesus change lives?
5. Can you prove God exists?
6. Why do bad things happen to good people?
7. Is there an alternative to violence?
8. You choose what works for you –
   I'll choose what works for me. OK?

WHAT IS SHOCK TACTICS: a flash from the future?

The year is 2010. And the world is changing fast.

It is an exciting time to be young. I don't just mean in the United States, where Macaulay Culkin is the youngest ever republican candidate to run for president. There is a general feeling everywhere that this is a good time to be born. In yesterday's newspaper, *The Daily Smut,* there was a photograph of Oasis with their newly-born grandchildren. The group were popular with young people in the early 90s and are still available to replay their old hits at nostalgia gigs, wedding receptions and pensioners' nights.

The political world has changed a great deal. There have never been so many changes of Prime Minister at any other period in history. Lord Geldof of Boomtown's six months in the post may not seem a very long stretch, but at least he was popular. The woman who followed him tried to solve the jobs crisis by taxing unemployment. That was disastrous! After that it was the schools' turn to suffer. But then, whoever had the stupid idea that young people would want to learn more if the Secretary of State for Education was Noel Edmonds? Now that health service reforms mean operations are performed only by national lottery, the present government is bound to fall.

The country's sporting performance continues to be a source of frustration. Having said that, the national football team has just seen an upturn with a very satisfying nil-nil draw – against the Galapagos Islands! It is seen as an important result, because a loss would almost certainly have led to the sacking of manager Sir Vinnie Jones. There is much debate as to what has gone wrong. Some blame the money which has flooded into the game, now that professional athletes compete for millions of euros. Others blame 3-D eye-operated computer games, which encourage children to sit around putting on flab instead of doing sport. That's ridiculous, of course! Just think how we have leapt forward in the only sport of which we are now world champions. Sumo wrestling!

The full might of science and technology have focused on solving the crisis of not being able to produce enough food to satisfy the multiplying population. The experimental programme that has produced pigs half the size of dinosaurs is still being perfected. *The Daily Smut,* who never miss a headline opportunity, demanded research into its possible beneficial effects for the human anatomy, with a front page splash headed 'Jurassic Pork'. The scheme has guaranteed the availability of food for this country until next century, but as ever, the benefits go to the rich nations, while the poor struggle for rights.

Global warming may have led to such tropical weather that jet-setters in search of sun and glamour now head for Margate, Blackpool and Ayr. But just look what it has done to Africa! No, don't look! Experience it in your own home on a virtual reality 'See it and be it' CD. This new form of entertainment offers you conscience-free escapism. In the comfort of your armchair you can tour the world in minutes, enjoying its spectacle and richness, with all the unpleasantness, suffering and anything that would provoke guilt edited clean away.

It is difficult to decide whether or not this has been a good decade for the church. The numbers of people attending have remained very much the same. The appointment of the new archbishop was a controversial one. Some say it is the reason why the church has succeeded in holding its numbers, few as they are. Others say it is the reason why the church hasn't grown more. Well, Cliff Richard always did divide people!

Your own church, though, has had a splendid year. The youth group is full of young people, and you are thoroughly proud of them. It is growing more and more inclusive – a place where rich and poor, black and white, intelligent and struggling, joyful and confused, female and male, insiders and outsiders, charming and downright awkward, meet on equal terms. You were thrilled by the extension especially for the young which was added to the church building last year. There was a great deal of excitement and hope at the opening ceremony, which was graciously conducted by Mrs Liz Windsor, much loved ex-queen of the Commonwealth, now executive director of UK Monarchy plc.

The youth group never fails to offer something stimulating – drama, discussion, Bible study, creative group work, prayer and praise of a most imaginative kind, and talks that deal with day-to-day life. The faces of the young people in 2010 don't look so very different from the ones you know. In fact, it looks as if they are about to begin their meeting. Come inside!

HOW TO USE SHOCK TACTICS

Each chapter of Shock Tactics is made up of the same six sections

1 SHOCK drama

A sketch set either in a future age or which is in some way timeless or surreal. Each has between one and five characters and very simple requirements for scenery or props. The drama's function is not to teach, but to raise issues.

2 short sharp SHOCK

A case study for the young people to discuss in small groups. It is explained as if the date is 2010, and describes an ethical dilemma which young Christians in that year may be facing. Although the situations are imaginary, they are all extreme developments of things which are beginning to emerge as possibilities even now. In reality, of course, the young people will be talking about things that are directly relevant to their own lives and experience. The reason for setting them in the future is that, by doing so, the young people are free to discuss things without the hang-ups and inhibitions brought about by their experience of present-day church, family, lifestyle or peer pressure.

The dilemma to be discussed should be read out loud, followed by the question. If the group is a large one, the young people should split into smaller groups for this activity – groups that they stay in for most of the rest of the programme.

These discussions are the key element of each chapter. Effort should be made to put them into tongue-in-cheek context by making a big fuss of transporting the group forward to the year 2010. The introductory part of this book, 'What is Shock Tactics?' could be read to give a humourous sense of something special about to happen.

3 bible SHOCK

A group study which takes the futuristic issues discussed by the young people and asks them to investigate how the Bible relates to that subject. There should be no need for a leader to act as convener for each group, since the questions are phrased in such a way as to enable young people to discuss them by themselves. Leaders who sit in on these groups should do so as participants, not directors. Each group will need one or more Bibles and a list of the questions.

4 SHOCK waves

A creative piece of work which asks the groups to communicate one element of what has emerged from the Bible study that they can all agree to and own. They are invited to present what they have decided in a variety of ways, each involving some kind of artistic response – a non-verbal one in the majority of cases. If there are a large number of young people, who have split into several smaller groups for these discussion activities, the creative responses are subsequently displayed so that the groups can compare each other's reactions in the context of worship.

5 SHOCK absorber

A portfolio of prayers, praise and acts of worship of various kinds, diverse enough to meet and extend the favoured styles of a wide range of traditions. Each chapter offers seven different styles of worship response:

- a selection of songs and hymns (the figure in brackets represents the volume in which the song was originally published)
- a way of using the Shock Waves responses worshipfully
- a led prayer with elevated language
- a responsive prayer in which the leader says alternate lines and the entire group responds with the repeated italic lines

- suggestions for spontaneous open prayer
- a silent reflection or meditation
- a creative prayer involving movement, symbolism, writing or drawing

6 talking SHOCK

An outline for a short talk or sermon, which brings everything that has been imagined in the future back to the present day. This is given not as a script to be read, but in 'pick and mix' note form ready for development in the style with which the speaker is most comfortable. There are also quotations from famous people, jokes, stories, statistics and song lyrics, given to weave into the talk in whatever way seems appropriate, so as to bring it to relevant life for the group.

The activities in each chapter can be put together in various ways to suit the needs of your own group:

A series of evenings

There is too much in each chapter to use in one evening. One way of fitting the material into a programme is to run a theme for three successive (perhaps weekly) evening meetings. To help you do this, the chapters are divided into three parts – the first is reasonably light-hearted, the second relates more closely to the Bible, and the third is a more customary blend of talk and prayer. For the youth group that adopts this approach, this book contains six months' worth of resources.

A weekend event

If the scheme is used at a residential or non-residential event, choose one of the chapters to follow through from Friday evening to Sunday lunchtime. The Friday evening should consist mainly of a social event, the climax of which is the performance of the drama. On Saturday morning, the stage should be set for transporting the group to the year 2010 by reading part of the introduction to this book – 'What is Shock Tactics?' The Short Sharp Shock discussion follows. After a mid-morning break, the Bible Shock section is used, and in the afternoon, Shock Waves. The evening features a 'futuristic' party or disco. On the Sunday morning there should be a service, structured to make best use of the suggestions for worship, the contributions of the young people in response to the Bible study, and the sermon.

An all-day event

In a group of two dozen or more, it is possible to use the entire book in one day with a great deal of choice by the young people as to what they want to get out of it. In these circumstances, the group should be divided into exactly eight smaller groups of at least three and at most about ten. Eight leaders (or older members of the group standing in as leaders) each take responsibility for one of the eight subjects in the book. They should have written on a card the Short Sharp Shock dilemma from their chapter. 'What is Future Shock?' is read. Then each leader goes to one of the groups and reads her or his futuristic dilemma. The group discusses this for five minutes precisely, and then a bell rings. The leaders get up and move on to the next group, circulating until each group has been visited by all eight leaders. After a break, the groups should decide, independently of each other, which of the eight subjects they want to study in more depth. The Bible Shock questions should be available so that they can look at the subject they have chosen. It doesn't matter if a subject is chosen by more than one group. The Shock Waves responses are presented in the usual way during an act of worship – although, of course, these will deal with several different subjects at the same time.

Mix and match

And, of course, if none of those three settings is suitable, resources from the chapters can be used independently of each other as part of an imaginative and integrated programme of activities for young people.

Aftershock

Many of the subjects that these chapters cover have the potential to inflame past hurts or to raise issues within members of the group which require a listening ear, one-to-one. So it is advisable to have experienced listeners ready to follow up any issues that emerge, and to develop an atmosphere in which young people are confident that non-judgemental pastoral care is available to them.

1 Issues concerned with... parents

PART 1

SHOCK drama

Some children do 'ave 'em!

CHARACTERS

- **Simon** (the son)
- **Anne** (the daughter)
- **Ron** (the father)
- **Elsie** (the mother)

Simon is marching angrily round and round a table, repeatedly looking at his watch. Anne sits nervously on the edge of a chair.

Simon: It's outrageous! I can't believe they've got the nerve to disobey us again. They've got no respect.

Anne: Just calm down, Simon. Try not to be too hard on them. There might be a perfectly valid reason for them being so late.

Simon: Oh Anne, you're far too soft on them, and you shouldn't believe everything they tell you. I wonder what gem of an excuse they'll come up with tonight. We've already had 'My watch stopped' and 'The train was late'. I offered to pick them up, but they wouldn't have it. 'Too embarrassing,' they said. 'Our friends will laugh at us,' they said. Well, this time I've had enough. They're not going to treat this house like a hotel any more. *(Thumps the table as the front door opens. Elsie and Ron tiptoe in, giggling. Their faces drop as they see Simon and Anne waiting.)*

Anne: Simon, stay calm.

Simon: Mother, Father, come here! *(Sarcastically.)* Well, well, well. Look who we have here. And exactly what time do you call this?

Ron: Um ... er ... Midnight, usually.

Simon: Don't try to be smart with me, old man! We told you to be home at 11 o'clock and no later. It's disgusting, people of your age being out at this time of night. You are our parents – you should be setting a good example.

Anne: Where have you been, anyway?

Ron & Elsie: *(Quickly and together.)* Nowhere.

Simon: I knew it! You've been down to that Conservative Club again, haven't you? *(Awkward silence.)* Speak to me when I ask you a question. Mother, have you been to the Conservative Club?

Elsie: *(Starts snivelling.)* Y ... yes.

Simon: *(Getting angrier by the minute.)* I knew it! After everything we've said. Why can't you go to the Bingo Hall like nice parents?

Elsie: It's not fair. Everyone else's children let their parents go there.

Anne: *(Puts her arm round Elsie.)* Don't cry, Mum. It's just that Simon and I want what's best for you. Besides which, I don't like that Mrs Jones you meet at political meetings – she's a bad influence on you.

Elsie: *(Indignantly.)* She is not!

Anne: Don't use that tone of voice with me, Mother. Just take a look at that awful outfit you're wearing – it proves my point. I might have guessed that when you and Mrs Jones went shopping she'd take you to Marks and Spencer. Why didn't you get changed like I asked you to?

Simon: *(Sniffing the air around Ron.)* What's that smell, Father? ... I don't believe it. After all we've said – you've been drinking Horlicks again, haven't you?

Ron: Well, um, only one.

Simon: When are you going to give me some respect and start listening to what I say? You won't catch us acting like this at your age. Just ... just get out of my sight before I do something that I regret.

Anne: I suggest you get straight into bed and make sure you're up early for church tomorrow.

Elsie: Oh no! Do we have to? I hate church. It's full of young people singing loud, modern songs. And the sermons are far too short. It's so irrelevant to your father and me.

Ron: I can't go anyway. I brought some work home from the office which I need to do by Monday.

Anne: Why do you always leave these things until the last minute? You should have done it on Friday night and got it out of the way.

Ron: But why?

Anne: Because ... because ... because I told you to. That's why! Don't argue.
(Elsie and Ron leave miserably.)

Simon: I can see we're just going to have to be stricter with them, Anne. This isn't the 1990s any more. Just because they had to obey their parents *then* doesn't mean they can live the wild life *now*. They are adults, for goodness sake! No, while we're living under their roof they'll have to do what we say. I'm going to have to start punishing them.
(They begin to move off, still talking.)

Anne: I know. We could ban them from watching *Coronation Street* – that would really upset them.

Simon: Or limit Mother's hair-dye allowance. She gets through far too much as it is.

Anne: That's a good idea. Oh Simon, it's so hard being somebody's children these days, don't you think?

short sharp SHOCK

To be announced to the whole group as a dilemma

When the Children Act (Amendment) was passed in 2001, teenagers quickly became used to having a new set of rights in law. If a parent gave a child a punishment he or she thought was unfair, the child was given access to the law courts to get justice. Your friend Lee was grounded for a week for coming in late after spending the evening playing table tennis with you.

For discussion in small groups:

As a Christian, will you go to court to give evidence against Lee's parents to try to get compensation for him?

PART 2

bible SHOCK

For discussion in small groups

1. Read Ephesians 6:1–4. The discussion you are going to have may touch a few raw nerves, so pray now that God will enable your conversation to be constructive, not negative, and that your family lives may be richer as a result.

2. Read verse 1 and verse 4 again. Notice how balanced they are. Although the principle is given 'so that all may go well', there are bound to be times when parents make demands that are exasperating or unwise to obey. In your experience, what has been your worst reaction to these demands (one that you would advise against anyone repeating)? What have you found to be a helpful reaction as far as long-term relationships are concerned?

3. Read Luke 2:41–52. Jesus was a typical baby, a typical child, and a typical teenager. That means parent problems were part of his experience. Here he is saying, 'I'm old enough now to be independent.' His parents are saying, 'That's what you think, young man, but we've got other ideas.' What strikes you as admirable about Jesus in these verses? What strikes you as admirable about his parents?

4. Read Proverbs 23:22–25. Think about your father, mother, or the adults who fill those roles for you. Try to identify specific positive benefits to do with wisdom, discipline and understanding which you have received from them one way or another over the years. See if each member of the group can name at least one thing.

5. Read verse 24 again. Then get someone to read it with 'she' instead of 'he', 'mother' instead of 'father', and so on. Make a list of potential flash points in family life (eg, the way you decorate your bedroom, the age at which you can have a boyfriend, etc). When the list is complete, work through it one point at a time, thinking of creative approaches to it which are 'righteous' (fair) and 'wise' from the point of view of the teenagers involved. Is there any hope that these could give 'joy and delight' to parents?

SHOCK waves

Materials: Large pieces of card or lining paper, scissors, felt markers, Blu-tack.

Working in small groups and using any of the materials provided, make a poster that expresses one of the things you have talked about concerning parents during this discussion. Cut the piece of card into a shape that represents the kind of home in which people in the group live (eg, a traditional house shape with a sloping roof, a tall, thin tower block, a terraced row of houses). In the body of the home, draw pin-men or blob-women to represent all the family arrangements which members of the group have (eg, single parent and child, two parents and several children, a large group living with house-parents). The names of the group should appear in the home as well. In the roof, the group should write a message about what they want God to do for the families represented on the poster – something the whole group agrees they want to say in the light of the Bible study.

ART 3

SHOCK absorber

Prayers and acts of praise in seven contrasting styles from which to choose

A selection of songs and hymns:

- A new commandment, *Songs of Fellowship* (3), *Mission Praise* (2)
- Father God I wonder, *Songs of Fellowship* (3), *Mission Praise* (2)
- Father, I place into Your hands, *Songs of Fellowship* (1), *Mission Praise* (1)
- I will change your name, *Songs of Fellowship* (4)
- Jesus put this song into our hearts, *Songs of Fellowship* (4), *Mission Praise* (2)
- Let there be love, *Songs of Fellowship* (1), *Mission Praise* (1)
- O Father of the fatherless, *Songs of Fellowship* (5)
- Peace I give to you, *Mission Praise* (2)

Using the Shock Waves responses

The posters should be displayed around the walls. Ask the group to get up and walk round the room in silence. They should pause in front of each poster to look at it and reflect on what it says and what it shows that the group who created it have learnt. They should use this as the basis of their own silent prayer, thanksgiving or making of promises to God – either about their own relationships with the adults with whom they live, or for the people who made the poster. After a silence (the length depending on how many posters there are for the group to examine) play some quiet music, which is the sign for the participants to retake their seats.

Led prayer

An ancient Scottish blessing:

Peace between neighbours,
Peace between kindred,
Peace between lovers,
In the love of the King of Life.
Peace between person and person,
Peace between wife and husband,
Peace between parent and child,
The peace of Christ above all peace. Amen.

Responsive prayer

Holy God, we confess to you the times when we have failed to treat those with whom we live with the care you expect of us.

For the things we say which hurt each other, perfect parent of us all,
Forgive us and help us, we pray.

For times when we insist on getting our own way. despite what others feel, perfect parent of us all,
Forgive us and help us, we pray.

For times when we increase the tension instead of seeking to make peace, perfect parent of us all,
Forgive us and help us, we pray.

For our anger, our lack of respect, our failure to listen, perfect parent of us all,
Forgive us and help us, we pray.

And because sometimes we just get bored with each other, perfect parent of us all,
Forgive us and help us, we pray.

Open prayer

Ask everyone to find a partner. Then ask each pair to join up with another pair to make fours. (Almost certainly there will be irregular sized groups of three or five – this does not matter.) A leader, timing this activity with a watch, should announce that each member of the group has thirty seconds to say something for which they are thankful about the people with whom they share their homes. Next, one after another, each has the same length of time to say one thing which they find difficult about the adults they live with or for which they need particular prayer. Ask people to make it clear if they are sharing things in confidence and don't want them repeated outside the group. In a time of open prayer, encourage the groups to pray for each other by name, mentioning the particular things which they have heard.

Silent reflection

Invite the group to shut their eyes and imagine themselves in their homes, using these words, and pausing in the places indicated:

All the usual activities of a weekend are going on – homework, housework, music, television, conversation, arguments, eating – each in the various rooms of the home ... There is a ring on the doorbell, and you go to answer it. It is Jesus! ... In your mind, invite him into your home. One by one, introduce him to each member of your family. If members of your family live away from your usual home, show him photographs. As you introduce him, tell him what your feelings are about the people he is meeting ...

Lord Jesus, may your love invade the places where we live, and may we always be aware, through good and bad times, of your presence there. Amen.

Creative prayer

Give everyone a square of coloured paper and ask them to fold the top corners back so that they make a traditional house shape. This represents the place in which they live (even if it does not look much like it!). In the 'roof' of the house they should write their name. In the body of the house they should draw themselves and the people they share their home with. They can go on to add details, such as the pets, furniture, things which are important parts of their bedroom, and so on. Somewhere in the house they should write, in as few words as possible, what they would like to pray for the household (eg, 'fewer arguments', 'more welcome for my friends', 'moving house', 'my grandmother who is ill'). Invite everyone to show their 'house' to the person sitting next to them, enjoy laughing at each other's sketches, explain what all the drawings are, and say why they have chosen the 'prayer' they wrote. While some music is played or songs are sung, the papers should be collected up and displayed with *Blu-tack* on a wall so that the prayers can be shared by anyone who wants to look at them.

talking SHOCK

Outline of a talk

At the time when the Bible was written, there was no such thing as a 'nuclear' family of mum, dad and kids in a little unit. Instead there were large extended families, all living in one household – parents, grandparents, children, children's wives, aunts and uncles, slaves, slaves' children, and so on. Many of the pressures on families today were less of a problem, because support was at hand and responsibilities were shared.

In that context, the Bible writes about two-way responsibilities between parents and children. In Colossians 3:20–21, Paul writes that parents should never embitter or discourage their children, and that children should obey their parents. It is spelt out elsewhere – hear your parents' point of view, make them proud of you, show them you appreciate what they do, even into old age (Proverbs 23:22–25). In return, parents were supposed to bring up their children to love God and to enjoy fully the wonderful life that God plans for his creation (Deuteronomy 6:1–7).

It did not always work out that way, and it still doesn't. The Bible is starkly realistic when it tells the stories of families – they were unkind to each other as often as kind, there were divorces as well as life-long faithfulness, there was abuse as well as sacrificial love, and emotional, forgiving reunions only happened because there were bust-ups in the first place. At no time did God stop loving any member of these families. He understands these things and he doesn't insist that children suffer passively and obediently. Not in extended families – and not in blended families, nuclear families, one-parent families or adopted families either.

Instead, the key to it all is one of the ten commandments: 'Respect your father and your mother, so that you may live a long time in the land that I am giving you' (Exodus 20:12). Respect can be seen as a matter of honouring the adults on whom (as a baby and child) you were once completely dependent, during the transition to the time when you become completely independent of them – and after! It is not the same as obeying without a hint of negotiation. It is not even the same as liking. But it should dictate the way we understand and relate to those adults, even if they have let us down in their responsibilities toward us. In the land that God has given us, society works best and stays stable if we can adapt that principle to whatever family set-up we find ourselves in.

Some stories, facts and quotations to help you

- *My main reason for wanting to be famous was so that my parents would be forced to notice me.*

Sting

- *Robert Bolt, the Oscar-winning playwright, was brought up in a strict Methodist family. His parents insisted that, until he was grown, he was to go to church with them without fail every Sunday. At the age of 16, his father said, 'You are an adult now. You must make your own choice whether or not you will carry on going to church.' Robert replied, 'I am never going again.' 'I see,' said his father. 'Then that is how it will be.' Robert's father never went again either.*

- *In September 1990, Helmut Klein took his son Andreas to the German high court. Why sue him? To force him to clear up the clothes, records, empty Coke cans and dirty plates in his room.*

- *Although my dad does not believe in Christianity, he says that whatever made me change is great. At first he went really mad when I tried to explain to him. Then when I turned around and said I was going to be baptised he went really off it. He wouldn't speak to me for days and I said, 'Well, you're not going to stop me. I feel it is right and I've got to do it.' So I went out and got baptised and I came back and now they are really accepting it. Now they'll not stop me from doing anything, even though it is against what they think.*

Christine (interviewed in Teenage Beliefs, David Day and Philip May, Lion Publishing, 1991)

- *25 per cent of all UK children experience the divorce of their parents.*

- *Only half of all children in Britain are expected to spend their entire childhood living with their married natural parents.*

- *Teenagers invariably involve growing old fast. For instance, between the ages of thirteen and nineteen you will probably notice your parents age by about thirty years.*

- *A woman had a teenage son who persistently had no interest whatever in Christianity. Every Sunday she would nag him, 'Won't you come to church with us?' And every day she would ask, 'Have you said your prayers today?' She put little tracts between his pillows when she changed the bed sheets and Bible verses under his sandwiches when he took a packed lunch. It was all to no avail. One day, in despair, she dropped to her knees and prayed fervently that whatever the obstacle was to her son becoming a Christian, God would take it away. There was a flash of lightning, and she completely disappeared!*

2 Issues concerned with... euthanasia

PART 1

SHOCK drama

Passing time

CHARACTERS

- **The man** (a mime, in jeans and T-shirt)
- **Male voice** (unseen)
- **Female voice** (unseen)
- **An arm** (appears from behind a screen)

PROPS

Seven watches in identical gift boxes
A walking stick

SETTING

An empty space beside a screen of some kind. All furniture and equipment is mimed, apart from the watches and walking stick.

The man walks on from behind the screen with the unsteady gait of a toddler. He drags a walking stick behind him like a plaything.

Male voice: Go on! Off you go! Just be good and play there for a little while. *(The man walks around and looks up and down. He is quickly bored. Looks upward as if at an adult much taller than he, reaches up and tugs at an imaginary sleeve.)*

Male voice: Not now, son, I said I was busy. *(The man toddles away and swings the walking stick, picks his nose, looks at it and flicks it at the audience. Laughs. Pulls at Dad's sleeve and points out what he has done.)*

Male voice: I said not now. Daddy's very busy indeed. Later. *(The man holds the walking stick upside down and kicks the handle. Turns round and scratches his bottom. Bends over and looks at the audience between his legs. Tries to look up at his bottom, then reaches up between his legs and scratches it with the walking stick. Laughs. Straightens up and tugs at sleeve to show Dad what he has done.)*

Male voice: No! That's naughty! I said not to disturb me and I meant it. *(Sound of a slap. The 'toddler' grabs his bottom, hurt. Juts out lower lip, very sulkily. An arm appears round the edge of the screen holding out a box. He takes and opens it. He is delighted with the watch inside and puts it on his wrist. Throws the box over his shoulder. He turns round in a full circle and stands in a more mature way as a teenager. He tucks the walking stick in the belt of his jeans.)*

Female voice: Great party, isn't it! *(The man nods and jives around – he's a terrible dancer.)*

Female voice: You're not very good at this, are you? *(The man shakes his head and smiles. Tries harder.)*

Female voice: Do you want to come outside for a bit? *(The man freezes. Looks sideways as if he can't quite believe it. Shrugs, pretending he's indifferent. Then rushes to the back of the space, ending with his back to the audience. He puts his left hand over his right shoulder and his right hand round the left side of his waist so that it looks as if someone else's arms are draped round him. He moves his hands up and down as if he's getting off, slowly at first then faster.)*

Female voice: Hmm! I've been wanting to do this ever since I got here. *(The man stops for a moment,* *pants, then starts again.)*

Female voice: Slowly! Slowly!
(He slows down for about three seconds, then goes even faster than before.)

Female voice: Ouch! What's that sticking in me?
(He looks down. It's the walking stick. He unhooks it, shrugs, hooks it in the back of his jeans instead, and goes back to speed-snogging.)

Female voice: Not so fast. Don't be greedy. We've got all the time in the world.
(The arm appears round the screen again with a box. The man drags himself away, takes the watch out of the box and, with delight, puts it on his wrist above the previous one. Throws the box away. He turns round in a full circle and looks more mature. Puts the walking stick over his left arm and rests his right hand on it.)

Male voice: Dearly beloved, we are gathered here...
(The man looks at the place where his bride's eyes would be if she were there.)

Male voice: Joined in holy matrimony...
(The man flutters his eyelids in a romantic way.)

Male voice: Do you take this woman?...
(The man nods frantically. The voice gets faster.)

Male voice: Richer, poorer, better, worse...
(The man looks at watch as if eager to get to reception. The voice gets faster still.)

Male voice: Sickness, health, forsaking all others, long as you both shall live...
(The man gestures to speed it up.)

Male voice: Love, honour, obey, who has the ring?...
(The man reaches out, sudden anxious look and gestures urgently. Phew! Takes imaginary ring and fits it on handle of walking stick. Voice is very fast.)

Male voice: With this ring, man, wife, no man put asunder, you may kiss the bride...
(The man grins and kisses the walking stick. The arm appears and the man repeats what has gone before with the third watch. Turning round, he faces the audience again with the stick in his arms, cradling it as if it were a baby.)

Female voice: *(Makes gurgling baby noises.)*
(The man looks down proudly, then smiles inanely – the proud dad. Then he catches sight of the TV in front of him and realises the football is on. Suddenly he isn't much interested in children.)

Male voice: ...and it's a magnificent pass from the half-way line by Sinclair. And Wilkins is there waiting for it. Look at him go – extraordinary for a man of his age. But Sinclair's there again. He's in the area and he's on-side. Where's the defence? There's no one to stop him. He's got masses of time. The crowd are going wild. The keeper stumbles. It's...
(As the commentary continues, the man gets more and more engrossed. Tries to give the baby away without taking his eyes off the TV, but there is no one to take it, so he has to hold it again. The baby is crying. He rocks it frantically. He mimes gesturing other children to get out of the way of the screen and cranes his neck around them. Whacks one of them to get him out of his line of vision, then pats him apologetically. The arm appears. He moves across to get the box, trying not to lose sight of the match. He goes through the usual procedure with the watch, and just as he is putting it on the commentary explodes...)

Male voice: It's a goal!
(The man has missed it! He is furious, scowling at the baby. Turns in a circle and comes to rest with the stick held vertically in one hand as a desk. He half sits and, with the other hand, begins to type, move the mouse of his computer, write letters, etc. He keeps picking up a telephone, more and more reluctant to be interrupted.)

Female voice: I have Mrs Brown in reception for you. You won't keep her waiting, will you?
(The man nods, but raises his eyebrows despairingly. Puts the phone down, and picks it up again almost immediately.)

Male voice: You're late for the product development meeting. You haven't forgotten it, have you?
(The man shakes head, sighs, puts down phone and writes faster. Phone goes again.)

Female voice: That was your wife on the phone. Why didn't you meet her for lunch. Did you forget it was your anniversary?
(The man mouths obscenity. Puts down phone. Wipes sweat off forehead. Picks up phone again.)

Male voice: I'm afraid we're offering the promotion to someone else. You had all the right qualifications, of course, but we felt time was running out for you.
(The man slams phone down in dismay. The arm appears and he dons the fifth watch. Turns around to face the audience, this time slightly slower on his feet with the stick in one hand being used for the first time as a walking stick.)

Female voice: Hallo Dad, nice to see you. We said we'd drive over and see you, didn't we? Doesn't time fly! Go on, James, kiss Grandpa.
(The man bends down, awkwardly.)

Female voice: Give Grandpa a kiss. I said *kiss* Grandpa or there will be no sweets today! Agh! Naughty boy! Right, early to bed for you, young man!

Male voice: We promised we'd come for your birthday! Many happy returns. I said, many happy returns!
(The man holds out his hand as if offering them a seat.)

Male voice: Oh I'm sorry, Dad, we can't stop. You know what it's like. Rush, rush, rush!

Female voice: We'll be seeing you again soon.
(The man waves sadly.)

Male voice: We'll try and stay longer next time. The video's broken down, you see, and you know what the kids are like if they miss *Neighbours!* Bye, bye!
(The arm presents the watch. The man hesitates before putting it on. He counts all six with a sigh. When he turns round this time, he is very frail, needing both hands on the stick to hold himself up.)

Female voice: Now, come on, take your medication like a good boy.
(The man swallows reluctantly.)

Female voice: There you are! That wasn't so bad, was it? I'll tell matron you've been a real Mr Brave. We're going to put you on a new course of treatment tomorrow. Add ten years to your life. That'll be good, won't it!
(The man looks up despondently, and is on the verge of shaking his head.)

Female voice: Now don't look like that! We don't want you to have a touch of the Mr Gloomies, do we? No, no, no! We're going to fight the old enemy Mr Coffin as long as we can, aren't we?
(The man shakes his head.)

Female voice: Dear oh dear! That won't do! You can't decide it's time to give up now. In fact, you can't decide anything anymore, can you?
(The arm comes out offering him the watch. The man pushes it away. The arm offers it again, more insistently.)

Female voice: Be a Mr Long-suffering. You know it's good for you. One more time.
(The man pushes the arm away again, but it won't go away.)

Female voice: Mr Long-suffering, Mr Long-suffering, Mr Long-suffering, Mr Long...
(As this is repeated, the man sinks to his knees, sliding down the stick.)

short sharp SHOCK

To be announced to the whole group as a dilemma

The Euthanasia Act (Amendment) of 2002 made provision for people who have a desire to end their lives. If they have a certificate signed by a psychiatrist and a doctor, and are not under pressure from a relative, they may sign into a Dignity Clinic to have a termination.

Christians have responded to this by forming Old Aid. They break into Dignity Clinics, handcuff themselves to people about to be terminated and swallow the key. In the two hours it takes for the police to come, they try to persuade the man or woman who was about to let themselves die that life is still worth living through Jesus.

For discussion in small groups:

Your friends have all worked for Old Aid. Will you?

ART 2

bible SHOCK

For discussion in small groups

❶ Read Leviticus 19:32. This study may rouse strong emotions in people – particularly if they have elderly relatives in mind. Pray that everyone will go through the discussion with respect for the elderly and the severely ill in every single contribution – and respect for each other too.

❷ Read 2 Samuel 19:31–39. This peaceful little story interrupts a dozen chapters of bloodshed in the stories of King David at war. Barzillai had shown David great kindness, and now David was in a position to return it. In what ways was what David offered (with the best will in the world) inappropriate? How did he come to respect what the old man wanted, rather than what he assumed the old man wanted?

❸ Read verse 37 again. Notice how very important it was to Barzillai that he died with his own dignity at a place and time he chose. This is very important to some old people. Is it possible to have a real respect for old people and yet deny them the right to make their own choices about their death? Secondly, is it possible to let people make decisions about the nature of their own death without defying the deep respect for life that Christians have?

❹ Read Psalm 88:1–18. This is the plea of an extremely sick man. It is similar to what some people say in despair toward the end of their lives – not only elderly people, but also those who have become severely disabled. On the surface the psalm reads like a plea for mercy-killing – can you find clues in it that the man secretly doesn't want euthanasia? If this person lived near your church, what could you as a group do practically, or persuade the authorities to do, to offer a real alternative to euthanasia, which would address the man's needs?

❺ Read Psalm 104:24-30. There are Christians who say that euthanasia is unacceptable because only God can have responsibility for giving and taking life, but who also press for the reintroduction of capital punishment and the maintenance of nuclear weapons to counter any attack by an enemy power. Does the fact that Christians believe there is an eternal life have any bearing on the way we think about these issues?

SHOCK waves

Materials: Large pieces of card or lining paper, a pile of magazines, scissors, paste, felt markers, Blu-tack.

Working in small groups, cut out, from the magazines, the faces of people of all ages and stages – babies to children to adults to elderly people. Arrange them on a page in a way that you think makes an interesting statement about the way we view people, the value we tend to put on human life, the way we treat the elderly, our attitudes to serious illness or euthanasia, or something similar that has struck you as you discussed the issue. (The group may find it difficult to find suitable pictures of elderly people, which is a statement in itself!) Add words if it helps. From your Bible study, choose a phrase that somebody used, or decide on one now, which summarises part of the discussion. Write it as a caption to the poster.

PART 3

SHOCK absorber

Prayers and acts of praise in seven contrasting styles from which to choose

A selection of songs and hymns:

- Give thanks, *Songs of Fellowship* (4)
- I am persuaded, *Songs of Fellowship* (4)
- Let it be to me, *Songs of Fellowship* (4)
- Light has dawned, *Songs of Fellowship* (4)
- My peace I give unto you, *Songs of Fellowship* (1), *Mission Praise* (2)
- We rest on Thee, *Mission Praise* (2), traditional hymn books
- You are my hiding place, *Songs of Fellowship* (2), *Mission Praise* (2)

Using the Shock Waves responses

The posters should be displayed around the walls. Ask the group to get up and walk round the room. They should pause in front of each poster to look at it and reflect on what it says and what it shows that the group who created it have learnt. They should use this as the basis of their own silent prayer – either for people they know personally or for those doctors, politicians, lawyers and relatives who make decisions about life and death. Some suitable contemporary music should be played to stimulate prayer, such as 'Low' (REM, *Out of Time*), 'Tears in Heaven' (Eric Clapton, *Unplugged*), or 'When will I ever learn to live in God' (Van Morrison, *Avalon Sunset*). The music stopping is a sign for the group to return to their seats.

Led prayer

O dear Christ who has known pain, uphold all those who endure suffering this day;
O dear Christ who has known fear, bring peace to all who are afraid this day;
O dear Christ who has known misery, be the strength of those who feel life has no purpose this day;
O dear Christ who has known desertion, be very close to all who face death this day in loneliness;
O dear Christ who has known death, be the hope of those who have no hope,
And in your mercy lead us all to the resurrection joy. Amen.

Responsive prayer

Everyone responds to the leader with the repeated italic line:

When I've only just been born,
While I feed or cry or yawn,
Fill me, Lord, with thanks to you.
When I've grown a little older,
And my toddling's getting bolder,
Fill me, Lord, with thanks to you.
In my school days as a child,
Through my learning, tears and smiles,
Fill me, Lord, with thanks to you.
In my teenages and youth,
Fall in love and search for truth,
Fill me, Lord, with thanks to you.
Growing through my middle life,
Parent, single, husband, wife,
Fill me, Lord, with thanks to you.

Then, as older years draw on,
Experience to call upon,
Fill me, Lord, with thanks to you.
Faithful through my Autumn days,
Looking back and full of praise,
Fill me, Lord, with thanks to you.
When my closing years are nearing,
Frail perhaps, but persevering,
Fill me, Lord, with thanks to you.

Open prayer

Ask the group to form pairs and share with each other what they feel they should be praying about following their investigation of this subject. Suggest that they might want to share in confidence information about people they know for whom, for some reason, this issue is urgent, and pray for them by name. Alternatively they could pray for those doctors, politicians and relatives who have to make extremely difficult decisions – and those who, without realising it, are having decisions made on their behalf. The prayer could also be for themselves, as they work out what they should think about this subject and face their own thoughts about illness and dying. Or they could agree just to stay silent and commit their thoughts privately to God. Suggest that the pairs talk for two or three minutes, and then pray just loud enough for their partner to hear.

Silent reflection

These words, an abridged version of Ecclesiastes 3:1–14, are read by a leader, pausing where indicated (…) for the group to dwell on the words:

Everything that happens in this world happens at the time God chooses. He sets the time for birth and the time for death … He sets the time for sorrow and the time for joy… The time for mourning and the time for dancing … The time for making love and the time for not making love, the time for kissing and the time for not kissing … He sets the time for love and the time for hate, the time for war and the time for peace, the time for silence and the time for talk …

What do we gain from all our work? I know the heavy burdens that God has laid on us. He has set the right time for everything. He has given us a desire to know the future, but never gives us the satisfaction of fully understanding what he does … I know that everything God does will last for ever. You can't add anything to it or take anything away from it … God does it so that humans will stand in awe of him … Let it be to me according to your word. Amen.

Creative prayer

On a low table in the centre of the room, place a number of night-lights (about twice the number as there are members of the group) in the shape of a cross. At the intersection of the cross should be a tall, lighted candle and a bowl of long-stemmed matches. Invite the group to pray the prayers that they haven't got words for by coming to the centre and lighting a night-light. They could light it as a symbolic prayer for a particular person, for people they do not even know the names of, for people who have no one else to pray for them, for whole communities and nations facing death – anyone whose predicament has been brought to mind by the subject. And, of course, they may light more than one candle. While the candles are being lit, play some music whose reflectiveness is appropriate to what is happening, such as 'Fragile' (Sting, *Nothing like the Sun*), 'Song for Guy' (Elton John, *Too Low for Zero* and compilation albums) or 'Exile' (Enya, *Watermark*). Let the activity take its own length of time, no matter how short or long that may be, and close it by fading out the music.

talking SHOCK

Outline of a talk

In Philippians 1:21–26, Paul wrestles with a decision – is he better off dead because he will be with Christ, or better off alive so that he can enjoy and serve the people he knows and loves on earth? If he asks the question, it must be OK for Christians to struggle with the same kinds of questions about dying.

The reason Christians can even dare to consider the possibility of euthanasia is because they can, in certain circumstances, look upon death as a friend. With the certainty of heaven before us, we can view death as a move from the world of the dying to the world of those who are truly and eternally alive. When one considers the alternatives – a human body growing ever more decrepit for eternity, or worsening suffering without any possibility of an end – this becomes easier to understand.

We know that God expects us to take a creative involvement in all the choices we make in service of him during this life. At every one of life's turning points, God wants us actively to choose his way. The question is, should choices about our own death be an exception – especially if it leads someone from suffering to paradise? Here Christian opinions differ.

What was Jesus attitude to death? In John 11:1–44 he hears terrible news – Lazarus, one of his closest friends, is severely ill. He insists that the timing of Lazarus' death is in God's hands and that God will be glorified through it (v4). He even waits for a while before going to the family (v6). At the moment he is confronted with Lazarus' death, Jesus is deeply upset (vs33–36). His tears fall even though he knows better than anyone that his own death would remove death's sting forever (vs 25–26). But notice the point at which he weeps – not when he hears that Lazarus is terminally ill, but when he is about to bring him back from paradise into the world of suffering where Lazarus is going to have to go through it all again.

How have circumstances changed since Jesus' time? The distress of being close to death, either your own or someone else's, has not changed. However, medicine and technology have given people the ability to live far beyond the point at which they would have died in a previous century (even the way in which death is defined is not as simple as it would have been in Jesus' day). Alongside that, the ability of doctors to control pain has advanced hugely, as has the provision of hospices where people can be fulfilled during their final days and face death with dignity. But don't forget that the temptation for a few people to manipulate their highly vulnerable relatives because of greed, anger or inconvenience is as strong today as it has ever been.

Some of these developments are reasons for Christians to resist euthanasia; some are reasons for Christians to look with sympathy toward those who are asking for help in coming to the end of their life. There is no simple conclusion to this talk, because there are no simple conclusions to the issue. However, here are some pointers to help us think in a Christian way about the issue:

- Don't fear death.
- Don't think it's wrong to be sad.
- Don't support euthanasia without first considering the terrible potential for abuse.
- Do support agencies and hospices which allow people to die with dignity and without pain.
- Do ask yourself whether there are limits on the way someone's suffering can 'bring glory to God'.
- Do recognise the difference between causing someone to die and allowing a natural death to take place because all that is left is an artificial life without any quality sustained by medical technology.

Some stories, facts and quotations to help you

- *There are three signs of growing old. The first is going grey, the second is losing your train of thought in mid sentence, and the third is … er…*
- *I have had much correspondence with the former chairman of the Euthanasia Society … and I took him round St Joseph's (hospice). He came away saying, 'I didn't know you could do it. If all patients died something like this we could disband the society.' If you relieve a person's pain and if you make him feel like a wanted person, then you are not going to be asked about euthanasia.*

Dame Cicely Saunders (founder of the hospice movement)

- *I don't want to achieve immortality through my work … I want to achieve it through not dying.*

The difference between sex and death is that with death you can do it alone and no one is going to make fun of you.

Dying is one of the few things that can be done just as easily lying down.

There will be no major solution to the suffering of mankind until we reach some understanding of who we are, what the purpose of creation was, what happens after death. Until these questions are resolved we are caught.

Woody Allen

• *We are pegging out in a very comfortless spot. Hoping this letter may be found and sent to you. I wrote you a word of farewell. I want you to think well of me and my end ... Goodbye – I am not at all afraid of the end, but sad to miss many a simple pleasure which I had planned for the future in our long marches. We are in a desperate state – feet frozen, etc, no fuel, and a long way from food, but it would do your heart good to be in our tent, to hear our songs and our cheery conversation ... We are very near the end. We did intend to finish ourselves when things proved like this, but we have decided to die naturally without.*

The final entry in the diary of Captain Robert Scott on his attempt to be the first person to reach the South Pole

• *Old man, exhausted by ordeal, detached from human deeds, feeling the approach of the eternal cold, but always watching in the shadows for the gleam of hope.*

President Charles de Gaulle describing himself

• *Strike that thick cloud of unknowing with the sharp dart of longing love, and on no account whatever think of giving up.*

The Cloud of Unknowing (an anonymous fourteenth-century devotional book)

• *There are only two kinds of people in the end: those who say to God, 'Thy will be done,' and those to whom God says, in the end, 'Thy will be done.'*

C S Lewis

• *The British parliament has debated, and rejected, legalising euthanasia four times in the last sixty years. In Australia and Holland the first terminations under new legislation took place in 1996.*

• *Sue Rodriguez, a Canadian woman who loved skiing, was diagnosed in August 1991 as having Lou Gehrig's disease, which brings progressive paralysis while the mind stays active. She campaigned for four years on television and in court to have medically-assisted suicides legalised – she maintained that denying them contravened the Charter of Rights. Her argument was always 'Whose body is this? Who owns my life?' She became a familiar public figure as she took her case to the Court of British Columbia (unsuccessfully) and then to appeal (unsuccessfully). As the country watched, she looked progressively frailer. In September 1993 she went to the Canadian supreme Court, which ruled against her by five judges to four.*

In the last days of her life, aged 43, she could not move, had to be spoon-fed, and every breath was a challenge. In January 1994 she told her husband Harry and her MP, Svend Robinson, that she had chosen to die on 12 February. She had dinner with her husband and nine year old son and they stayed until morning. An hour later the MP, who was a close friend, arrived with a doctor. The doctor administered a lethal injection, and Robinson held her in his arms for the rest of the morning. When she died peacefully, he called her palliative care doctor (a specialist in terminal illness, of whom there are many in Canada) and the police. Tearfully, he later told a press conference, 'She was so strong and courageous right up to the point she began to lose consciousness. She told me to relax at one point.'

After her death, the Canadian parliament were prompted to debate euthanasia. The Right to Die Society of Canada backs it, but opponents (among them many Christians) allege that the organisation manipulated a vulnerable woman for political ends. When asked how she wanted to be remembered, Sue Rodriguez replied, 'I want my son to be proud of me.'

3 Issues concerned with... sex

PART 1

SHOCK drama

Facts of life

CHARACTERS
• **Father**

PROPS
A guitar (propped up on a chair)
A catalogue of stringed instruments or a book of sheet music

The father is giving a lecture to his 'son' about the facts of life, but in the drama his talk is directed at the guitar. During the talk he veers from embarrassment to anger to pent-up frustration. Sometimes he is seated, sometimes pacing up and down.

Father: Now, son, I know you're wondering why I wanted to have this little chat with you tonight. I expect you're curious why Mum has gone out and left us. What could it be that's so awful that your old Mum can't hear, eh? Ha ha ha! Well, she and I have been talking and ... well ... we thought it was time you and I chatted away about ... things, really. The sorts of thing only you and I can talk about ... Man to, er, guitar!

Well, I guess you've noticed that not everybody is shaped the same. Some of us are guitar-shaped, but others are more – how can I put this – rounded. Not of course that I'm imagining you've had reason to notice. I mean, it's nothing to be ashamed of if you haven't, er ... I mean, in fact it's better if you didn't, um ... at least not until you are, ahem ... Look, let me put it this way! I never even saw your mother out of her case until we were engaged. And I can tell you, it was a pretty solid case too, none of your flimsy flop-overs that you see today, barely covering the sounding-board.

My goodness, times have changed since those days. I was twenty-one before I was allowed to touch her strings. And even then I had to promise it would just be the minor chords. Strumming was out of the question. We never got further than occasional fingers up and down the neck ... We never even dreamt of fretting!

So your mother and I decided ... this isn't embarrassing you, is it? ... Good! Your mum and I were having a chat and we thought that ... well, we love you very much, my boy, and *(voice raising slightly)* ... you see, we want the best for you and we've always tried our hardest to lead you in good taste *(louder)* and then today ... and then today ... *(holding up the book of music or guitar catalogue)* under your bed I discover this filth!

(Calming himself.) We want you to enjoy the nice things in life – Mozart ... Vivaldi ... Tammy Wynette. We want you to share your life with some lovely young violin – melodious, harmonious. But with you it suddenly seems like any old fiddle will do!

You see ... I know this seems hard to believe, but I was young like you once. I want you to have all the benefit of the mistakes I made. Just take care with that jolly old plectrum, my boy. And be sure you're ready for each new movement of the concerto.

I'm aware that people say it's safe as long as you've got a capo on. But it's not true! The only really safe duet is a life-long one ... Mind you, I'm not so thrilled about you going solo either ... And joining a group is out of the question!

So, I just want you to think about it this way. When you're alone with another instrument, you're never really alone. The King is always watching you ... Elvis! When you're tempted, you can always remember his words ... 'Don't be cruel to a heart that's true ... Love me tender ... Wop-bopaloola-da-wop-bam-boom ...' They'll help you keep your mind off the quavers. And the crochets!

Well, there you are! That wasn't so bad, was it? I'll leave you to mull it over. And you won't be surprised that I'm confiscating this.
(He walks off with the book catalogue, taking a sly look in it. His eyes widen and he turns it onto one side.) Goodness me! Why is it that a double bass springs to mind? *(Exit.)*

short sharp SHOCK

To be announced to the whole group as a dilemma

In 2003 the infallible condom for men and women was invented. The startling rise in sexually transmitted diseases led the government to pass a new act which meant that instead of school beginning with a daily act of Christian worship, it began with a daily act of sex education. These condoms were provided to schools to be handed out to everyone as they left the new assembly. On your way to biology, your friend William mentioned that now there is complete safety in sex, science has provided a wonderful escape from the boredom of having just one partner for life.

For discussion in small groups:

As a Christian, what do you say to him?

PART 2

bible SHOCK

For discussion in small groups

❶ Read 2 Samuel 13:1–22. This is a startlingly explicit passage, so you might like to pray first that you can talk about this subject honestly, but without getting embarrassed.

❷ Read verse 13 again. Tamar said, 'Wait until we're married.' It's the attitude that Christians have had down the centuries. What are the arguments in favour of waiting? Have new developments in science, medicine and ways of life meant that there are now viable arguments against waiting?

❸ Read verse 5 again. Jonadab said, 'I'll find a way for you.' What ways do people today use to try to coax people into sexual activity that they don't completely want?

❹ Read verse 15 again. Amnon hated Tamar after the rape more than he had loved or lusted after her before. This must be one of the most distressing verses in the whole Bible. When people use force in order to have sex, is what they do driven by hate, love or lust?

❺ Read verse 20 again. Absalom said, 'You're making too much out of something that's not important.' The way some Christians talk against sex you would think chastity is the only important thing about their faith. Have we got it out of proportion?

SHOCK waves

Materials: Large pieces of card or lining paper divided into two sections by a vertical line – one side is captioned, 'Do not conform yourselves to the standards of this world...' and the other side, '...but let God transform you inwardly' (Romans 12:2); a pile of girls' and women's weekly magazines and men's quarterlies, scissors, paste, Blu-tack.

Working in pairs or threes, create a montage by cutting and pasting images and headlines from the magazines. On the side that says, 'Do not conform yourselves to the standards of this world...' show something that the group believes not to be true, even though the magazine may encourage it. On the side that says '... but let God transform you inwardly', put something the group thinks is true. It is up to the group whether or not God is mentioned on the poster, but the sentiments should rise out of the Bible study, and it should be an honest statement. If necessary, words and pictures can be hand-drawn in felt marker.

SHOCK absorber

Prayers and acts of praise in seven contrasting styles from which to choose

A selection of songs and hymns:

- Father, I place into Your hands, *Songs of Fellowship* (1), *Mission Praise* (1)
- Here is love, *Songs of Fellowship* (4)
- Here we are, *Songs of Fellowship* (4)
- Let it be to me, *Songs of Fellowship* (4)
- Lord, look upon my need, *Songs of Fellowship* (5)
- Purify my heart, *New Songs (92/93)*
- Reign in me, *Songs of Fellowship* (4), *Mission Praise* (2)
- Such love, *Songs of Fellowship* (4)
- Teach me Your way, O Lord, *Songs of Fellowship* (4)
- We are moving on, *Songs of Fellowship* (1), *Mission Praise* (2)

Using the Shock Waves responses

The posters should be displayed around the walls. Ask the group, while instrumental music plays, to get up and walk round the room. They should pause in front of each poster to look at it and reflect on what it says, working out why the group believed some things to be true and some lies. They should use this as the basis of their own silent prayer, being honest to God about their reaction to the posters, and how they feel about the standards he sets. After some time, fade the music, which is the sign for the participants to retake their seats.

Led prayer

Lord God, I'm ashamed of this newspaper.
It only cost a few pence
and tonight it will lie in countless rubbish bins, forgotten.

It had the story of an MP's affair,
gossiped over by bored women.
It had a photo of a naked woman,
drooled over by boozing men.
It had tales of lurid sex,
condemned in one sentence and spiced up in the next.
It had jokes and double meanings,
leered at by under-used minds.
It had phone numbers promising a good time,
lusted over by lonely strangers.

Lord, when you chose to come to earth in person,
to be born in human skin,
to share all the strokes and thrills and discomforts of a human body,
Did you ever imagine it would come to this?

Well ... I suppose you did.

Lord God, I pray for all those whose lives are damaged tonight by sex:
Those who featured in this newspaper,
who can't throw away the hurt along with the newsprint;
And those whose hurt is still to come,
cut-price victims of the cheapness this paper gives to sex.

Lord God, I pray for all those whose lives are enriched tonight by sex:
Those whose hands and kisses say what words cannot, who find a living joy in unselfish giving;
Those whose intimacy will bring them closer than the atoms,
at one for ever in learning love and growing commitment.

What dignity you gave the human body by choosing to inhabit it!

Holy Lord, I ask now that I may use my body,
and the bodies of those I will love,
In such a way that you will find in them an honourable home,
And we will find in them a touch of heaven.

Through Jesus Christ our friend. Amen.

Responsive prayer

On those who want to please you, but find temptation great,
Have mercy, loving Lord,
Hold us all in your love.

On those who wonder why no one seems attracted to them,
Have mercy, loving Lord,
Hold us all in your love.

On those who have been wounded by sex they did not want,
Have mercy, loving Lord,
Hold us all in your love.

On those who have done things they wish they had not done,
Have mercy, loving Lord,
Hold us all in your love.

On those who are confused about what their sexuality makes them feel,
Have mercy, loving Lord,
Hold us all in your love.

On those with HIV or AIDS,
Have mercy, loving Lord,
Hold us all in your love.

On those who are pregnant and do not want to be,
Have mercy, loving Lord,
Hold us all in your love.

On all of us who want sex to be a rich joy in our lives,
Have mercy, loving Lord,
Hold us all in your love. Amen.

Open prayer

Invite those present to get into a small group with people they will feel comfortable praying with – that means with their friends, with strangers, in a pair with a boyfriend or girlfriend, alone, with a leader – the choice is theirs. On a chart display these adjectives:

encouraged
threatened
guilty
happy
embarrassed
jealous
indignant
frustrated
anxious
impatient
in love
regretful
at ease
irrelevant
emotional

joyful
thoughtful
cool
exhilarated
helped
tearful
thankful
jokey
lucky
secret
cheerful
content
scornful
in disagreement

Suggest that everyone chooses one word which describes how they feel about what they have been discussing. They should tell the rest of the group what word they chose – or a word not on the list if none of these adjectives get close to describing their real feelings. If they want to, they can go on to explain more of their thoughts about the subject, but nobody has to. They should then pray for each other, in as much or as little detail as has been revealed.

Silent reflection

This is a guided meditation which, with careful introduction and pacing, can be a liberating way of meeting God (but which also has a potential for giggling which may make it unsuitable for some groups). There should be silence in the places indicated (…)

Invite the group to shut their eyes and hold one of their hands in the other. Explain to them that they are to imagine that the hand they are holding belongs to several different people, and that they should silently tell these others what they are thinking.

First it is the hand of someone you find attractive – imagine yourself telling him or her what you think is the right and moral way forward for you …

Then it is the hand of yourself as a child – tell the young 'you' things you have since found out about sex that you wish you had known in advance …

Next it is someone whose face you can't see who will one day be your permanent partner – try to make him or her some promises about what will happen between now and then …

After that, it is Jesus' hand – explain to him the things that are difficult to explain to others. In fact you don't even need to put it into words, because he knows already, so just let him support you in those things …

Finally it is your own hand – be honest with yourself about how you feel about: the thought of being alone, your own sexual experience, what you will do about the advice you have heard …

Lord Jesus, in your mercy, hear and help us. Amen.

Creative prayer

Give an opportunity for everyone, completely confidentially, to write a letter to God explaining how they feel about what they have discussed, the difference (if there was any) between this conversation and others they have had about sex, their own experience (either rejoiced in or regretted), their hopes for themselves, and their fears for the future. Provide envelopes, as well as pens and paper, so that the letter can be sealed and taken away, for each writer to keep for reference or dispose of.

talking SHOCK

Outline of a talk

Sex is good! Don't be misled by rumours that God is anti-sex – he means it to be enjoyed! A whole book of the Bible, Song of Songs, is devoted to celebrating sex. It joyfully approves romantic dreaming, admiring the body of someone you love, kissing, and enjoying touch (both when it is loving and when it is simply affectionate and encouraging). Song of Songs 5:2–5 and 9–16 gives a good example.

However, the Bible is also clear that sex can be abused and used to hurt (2 Samuel 13:1–22). The world often treats sex cheaply – it is flaunted to sell things in adverts, portrayed as a giggle in tabloid newspapers, used by evil people who get rich by trapping youngsters into pornography or prostitution. Christians believe the world deserves better.

In God's eyes, sexual intercourse joins people together in every way – physically, emotionally, spiritually, permanently. This is why he intends that intercourse should be between one man and one woman who are married to each other (Matthew 19:4–6). Christians have always recommended young people to hold back some of their sexual experience and wait to have intercourse until they are ready to say to someone they love, 'I'm committed to you alone for the rest of my life.' Why? Because it pleases God that humans should live in the good way he intended.

It's obvious that God designed human bodies to be monogamous. The main reason AIDS and VD have spread so alarmingly is because people are using their sexuality in a way that their bodies were not created to handle. And God means pregnancy to be a matter of joy that will bring stability to a marriage, not disaster leading to anguish and agonising decisions (1 Thessalonians 4:3–7).

What if we feel we have let God down? (All of us have done – mentally if not physically.) God is able and longing to forgive us totally. He can never give back virginity to someone who wishes he or she still had it, but he can give back complete purity (1 John 1:9). Just ask him!

Is it impossible to be moral about sex in this day and age? No, just incredibly difficult! Remember Jesus' example. As a teenage boy he was human in every way, from wet dreams to raging hormones, but he not only resisted temptation, he also found himself completely fulfilled in being celibate (Hebrews 4:15–16). There's no one better to ask for help!

Some stories, facts and quotations to help you

- *The youth leader was completely discouraged by the fact that his youth club looked bored and fidgety during his meetings. He wondered if he might as well stop bothering. 'Whatever am I going to do?' he moaned to his wife. 'I might as well preach about taking the dog for a walk – they wouldn't even notice what I was talking about.'*

  'But you don't know anything about dogs,' replied his wife. 'It's me who takes Tolly round the park every day.' And that was the last he saw of her that weekend. He lovingly kissed her goodbye as she went off to look after her ailing mother for a couple of days.

  In fact it was that kiss which put an idea into the guy's head. Suddenly he knew how he would startle the teenagers into listening. He would speak about something urgently relevant, he would be outspoken, practical and honest – he would talk about sex! And that's what he did. It was brilliant – funny, touching, moral, followed by discussion – everything a good talk should be. In fact it was so helpful that one of the girls felt she had to phone up his wife as soon as she got home. 'It was a great meeting,' she said. 'Really helpful, and such a good choice of subject.'

  'Well, you amaze me,' said the wife. 'To be honest, I thought he had chosen a disastrous subject. In fact, he's only done it twice. The first time he got bitten on the leg, and the second time he got breathless and had to come home.'

• *I was best man to a good friend, and he stayed at my flat overnight after the stag party so that we could go down to the church together. I took him an early-morning cup of tea while he was in the bath. 'Hey, I've just been thinking,' he laughed, 'This is my last bath as a virgin.' That really tickled me, so after a brilliant service and a very formal reception, I decided during the evening disco to tell his wife what he had said. She looked at him, standing there with sweat cascading down his shirt and the unmistakable, wafting smell of over-energetic dancing in a small room, and she declared, 'That was not your last bath as a virgin!'*
Peter Graystone

• *Some people need cheap sex, instant selfish gratification. Fine! But it makes me more miserable than ever.*
Barry Lydon (aka Johnny Rotten of the Sex Pistols)

In 1992, of teenagers between 14 and 18 surveyed:

• *13% thought sexual intercourse before marriage is wrong.*

• *53% thought that living with someone was as good as marrying them.*

• *When asked how much they accepted of what their religion teaches about sex: 23% said nothing, 20% said not much, 18% said some, 9% said most of it, 6% said all of it, but 24% did not know what the teaching of their religion was about sex.*

• *I would do anything for love (but I won't do that).*
Meatloaf's chart-topping song

From a teenage magazine:

• *Dear Agony Aunt, I have been dating two girls and having good sex with both. However, they have both found out about each other and broken off the relationship with me. I am desperate and don't know what to do. Don't give me any of that morality jazz, but help!*
Discouraged of Manchester.
Dear Discouraged, the basic difference between man and animals is morality, so if you don't want any then I suggest you go and see a vet.

• *I haven't yet been able to find a happy adulterer.*
Tamasin Day-Lewis (producer of a Channel documentary series on adultery)

From page 2 of 'The Sun' newspaper, January 1994:

• *'Men who watch porn films are four times as likely to become impotent – because they get bored by sex thrills,' Italian sex expert Andrea Dotti warned yesterday.*

From page 3, the facing page of the same newspaper on the same day, underneath a rear view of a naked woman:

• *'Pud looking – Wendy Slingsby, 19, likes making desserts. But she never trifles with flans. So here's a nice pieful from the Dorset lass – best served without topping!'* No comment required!

4 Issues concerned with... the environment

PART 1

SHOCK drama

The World Samaritan

CHARACTERS

- **Narrator**
- **'The world'**
- **Three robbers** (who could also double as...)
- **Politician**
- **Industrialist**
- **Christian**

As the narrator speaks, the other characters mime what is being said. But the action becomes more confused when the parallels with the parable of the good Samaritan break down.

Narrator: There was once a world which was happy and healthy. She had a smile so big it stretched from Jerusalem to Jericho. One day, as she was going down the road, robbers attacked her, stripped her and beat her up. Her rivers and seas had chemicals poured into them. Her trees and foliage were ripped out by the roots. Her protective layer was punctured leaving her open to danger and abuse. *(All this is mimed by the robbers.)*

Narrator: The attack went on and on. Then she was left half dead. There seemed no hope for the world at all. It so happened that a politician was going down the same road. 'Aha!' she said. 'A dying world! This could help me win an election.' So she spent a tiny amount of her enormous budget on trying to make the world look better. But sadly the pressures of political survival pressed hard upon her, and before long something else caught her attention, and she walked on by on the other side. *(During the narration the politician mimes getting out some make-up and applying it to the world's face. She then leaves, putting a pennant in the world's hand, saying 'Vote for me'.)*

Narrator: In the same way, a head of industry came along. She ran a huge business, and couldn't help noticing the dying planet. She looked quite concerned, as if she wanted to make a real attempt to help. 'If we tell people that we help the world,' she said, 'they will be so impressed that they will buy heaps of our products.' So she had some labels saying 'Recyclable' made and stuck them all over the world. But after a little while, the labels got too expensive to produce, so she stopped. And to be honest, it didn't matter anyway, because she hadn't stopped pouring chemicals into the sea. And the world just got sicker as she walked on by on the other side. *(The industrialist mimes sticking self-adhesive labels all over the world's body. Just before she goes, she looks furtively round, then kicks the world with the back of her heel.)*

Narrator: But a Christian who was travelling that way came upon the world. When she saw the terrible state the world was in, she was outraged. The beautiful, fruitful world God had created had been attacked and was dying. When she saw the world, her heart was filled with pity: 'How could they have done this to you?' Then, suddenly, she saw the time! 'Quick,' she said. 'I'll be late for the prayer meeting. I'll be praying for you all evening, world. God will rescue you in the end.' And she walked on by on the other side. *(Christian mimes coming and going.)*

Narrator: So the world wasted away until eventually she died, and at the end...

World: *(Sitting up.)* Hang on!

Narrator: What?

World: That's not how it ends!

Narrator: It's in my script!

World: I know this story. It doesn't end like that! You get the Christian bandaging the world's wounds, putting her on a donkey, taking her to a hospital, and it all works out fine. It's in the Bible. I've seen it!

Narrator: I'm sorry, but here's the script. *(Shows it to actor.)* Narrator leaves, Christian prays, world dies, end of sketch.

World: It can't finish like that. I won't let it happen.

Narrator: We'll have to go by the script. Get back down on the floor.

World: *(Reluctantly lies down again.)* Well, I will as a favour to you. But I don't like it!

Narrator: We none of us like it. But that's the way it is in the real world. I've lost my place now! *(Looks at script.)* Here we are. The story-teller asked, 'Which one was truly a neighbour to the world? Which one really helped her?' But by this stage the world was too weak to answer. 'Go thou and do likewise,' said the story-teller, hoping with all his heart that they wouldn't.

short sharp SHOCK

To be announced to the whole group as a dilemma

In 2004 the full extent of the damage to the world's forests became clear, and one of the results was emergency restrictions on the use of paper for books. In a dramatic piece of legislation, best-selling books were rationed. For instance, only one Bible (the world's best-seller) was allowed per household. Export of books in foreign languages was banned, which was disastrous for Bible translators, since it meant that overseas mission and evangelism, which involved translation of Christian material into foreign languages, became illegal. The missionary societies were outraged.

For discussion in small groups:

Whose side are you on –
the environmentalists or the Christians?

ART 2

bible SHOCK

For discussion in small groups

1. Read Genesis 1:26–28 and 2:15–17. Pray that God will use your discussion in a way that practically makes a difference to your lives, and not just in a way that makes you despair for the earth.
2. Read 1:28 again. What is the difference between 'subduing' the earth, which God commands here, and 'dominating' the earth, which has led to such environmental abuse?
3. Read 2:15 again. What are the modern-day equivalents of 'working the earth' and 'taking care of it' (literally, 'guarding' it)? Make a list of things you see being done that are of value in those areas.
4. The Old Testament Law was not only the religious law, it was the national law-of-the-land as well. It has a reputation of being acutely environment-sensitive. Look up the following verses and work out why they would be beneficial to the environment – Deuteronomy 20:19–20; 22:6–7; 23:12–13 (no giggling, it's serious), 24:19–21; 25:4.
5. Read Colossians 1:15–16. There is something distinctive about the way Christians look at the environment, rather than any other good citizen. They believe that the earth was not only made through Christ, but was also made for him. It does not belong to humans; it belongs to Christ. What difference should that make practically to a Christian's actions? What difference should it make to the way we try to influence others – including those who do not recognise Christ to be the earth's owner?

SHOCK waves

Materials: Large pieces of card or lining paper, scissors, felt markers, paints, brushes, Blu-tack.

Working in small groups, think through the practical instructions for the protection of the environment which were given in the verses from Deuteronomy. Devise a present-day 'law' which is a modern equivalent – as many points as you like. The laws would be both religious and national, so they are not just for Christians, they are for everyone. And they should be as specific as the ones in the Bible. Using any of the materials provided, make a public information poster of the kind a government department might make to draw attention to the new 'laws', listing them and illustrating them in an eye-catching way.

PART 3

SHOCK absorber

Prayers and acts of praise in seven contrasting styles from which to choose

A selection of songs and hymns:

- All around me, Lord, *Mission Praise* (1)
- For the beauty of the earth, *Mission Praise* (2)
- God is our strength and refuge, *Mission Praise* (2)
- Jesus is Lord, *Songs of Fellowship* (1), *Mission Praise* (1)
- Jesus, Lord of everything, *Songs of Fellowship* (3)
- Restore, O Lord, *Songs of Fellowship* (2), *Mission Praise* (1)
- The Lord is a mighty King, *Songs of Fellowship* (4)

Using the Shock Waves responses

The posters should be displayed around the walls. Ask the group to get up and walk round the room. They should pause in front of each poster to reflect on what it says and what it shows that the group who created it want to communicate from their Bible study. They should use this as a way of making resolutions before God about changes they feel they need to make personally, and of praying to him for a world-wide change of heart of governments and nations. While they are doing this, play 'Emergency on Planet Earth', the title track from the Jamiroquai album. The end of the music is the sign for them to retake their seats.

Led prayer

The Canticle of the Sun, by Francis of Assisi:

Be praised, my Lord, by all your creatures.

And first by brother sun,
who makes the day bright and luminous.
He is beautiful and radiant
with great splendour:
He is the image of you, most high.

Be praised, my Lord, by sister moon and the stars.
You placed them in the sky,
so bright and twinkling.

Be praised, my Lord, by brother wind,
by the air and the clouds
and the airy skies
and every kind of weather,
through which you give nourishment
to all your creatures.

Be praised, my Lord, by sister water,
who is very useful
and humble and precious and pure.

Be praised, my Lord, by brother fire
who illuminates the night.
He is beautiful and joyous,
robust and strong.

Be praised, my Lord, by our sister, mother earth,
who keeps us and watches us
and brings fruit and grain of all kinds,
multicoloured flowers and herbs.

Be praised, my Lord, by our sister
the death of the body,
from which no one escapes.

Blessed are those who are found
doing your most holy will,
for death will do them no harm.

Praise and bless the Lord,
and give thanks to him,
and serve him with great humility.

Responsive prayer

God has filled the earth with beauty,
All the world give God your praises.

Worship is your joy and duty,
All the world give God your praises.

Who filled up the sea with water?
All the world give God your praises.

Made each child a son or daughter?
All the world give God your praises.

Made cows moo and set snakes hissing?
All the world give God your praises.

Who invented hugs and kissing?
All the world give God your praises.

Who decided stars would twinkle?
All the world give God your praises.

Eyes would wink and foreheads wrinkle?
All the world give God your praises.

Whose idea were films and telly?
All the world give God your praises.

Who makes Stilton cheese so smelly?
All the world give God your praises.

Only God could be that clever,
All the world give God your praises.

Let his praises sound for ever,
All the world give God your praises.

Open prayer

Invite the group to offer short prayers – one word or one sentence – in praise of God for one thing that they find amazing and beautiful in his created world. It could mean thanking God for beautiful sunsets, or wondering at Ayers Rock. At the end, the leader should close by praising God for the imagination that brought these things into being, and asking that we may have the creative imagination to enjoy them wisely and protect them.

Silent reflection

Play a sufficient extract of 'Is this the world we created?' by Queen, from the album The Works, to establish the mood and theme of the time of prayer, then reduce the volume. Over the top of it read these words:

Forgive, O Lord, the greed that damages tomorrow's world to comfort today's;

The laziness that litters tomorrow's world to ease today's;

The lack of care that pollutes tomorrow's world to convenience today's;

The ignorance that over-populates tomorrow's world to placate today's;

The injustice that deprives tomorrow's world to enrich today's;

The stupidity that forgets tomorrow's world and lives for today's.

Lord, have mercy,
Lord, have mercy,
Lord, have mercy.

If there is sufficient time, raise the volume until the end of the track, then have a time of silence. After a minute or so, read these words:

The Lord of all mercy will forgive us,
The Lord of all compassion will restore us,
The Lord of today's world and tomorrow's challenges us to change.

So be it!

Creative prayer

Distribute self-adhesive labels and pens. Invite the group, working individually or in pairs, to consider what they most want to say to God as a result of these sessions. They should write their prayers on their labels. When all have finished this, music is played while a globe (a small one on a stand or an inflatable one) is passed round the group. Everyone who wants to has the opportunity, one after the other, to attach their prayer to the globe. When it reaches the front of the room again, the leader should take the globe and place it in front of a cross (a free-standing one, or one cut from coloured paper and attached to a wall). He or she should use these words:

Jesus, Lord of Creation, we acknowledge that this planet is not ours, but yours. May we be aware of your world and the things which harm it. May we be agents of change – first changing small things, then changing our lifestyles, then changing the hearts of those in authority. May the cross that towers over the world be our forgiveness, our healing, and our help. Amen.

talking SHOCK

Outline of a talk

The first chapter of the Bible shows the basis of ecology – a world in delicate balance. Here can be seen God's order in creation, symmetrically balancing day and night, light and dark, water and land, work and rest – every part relying on every other part. Day one has echoes in day four, day two in day five, day three in day six. Utterly good and beautiful (Genesis 1:1–31)!

God made a world of great abundance, and then extravagantly gave humans the right to name everything and maintain control over it (Genesis 2:15, 20). This is an honour which is not to be taken lightly. Control brings the responsibility of maintaining God's ecology. Much of the damage that has been done to the world since the Industrial Revolution has been done in ignorance – and God is a forgiving God. But now we have the technology to monitor the damage and predict its effect on our future. Today we know! Today there is no excuse!

Our universe was created to be free, but the sins of humankind have injured the whole of creation. St Paul writes in the Bible that if a sterile, polluted lake had emotions, it would be frustrated. If a decaying, depleted ozone layer had a voice, it would be groaning. Creation is longing 'on tiptoe' for the day when God will intervene to put right all that is wrong and renew this ravaged earth (Romans 8:18–23). That is what we mean when we pray: 'Your Kingdom come'. What is needed is nothing short of world-wide repentance – literally 'a turning around'. But for the world to turn away from sin, it needs to start with me!

Christians know that this wonderful earth God has created does not belong to us; it belongs to Christ. It was made by him and through him. At the end of time, when God steps in to judge what has been wrong and remake the world in perfection, the entire created order will be given to the Lord Jesus Christ as his own (Colossians 1:15–20). He will ask, 'What did you do to guard and cultivate the planet I left you in charge of?' How feeble will your excuse sound?

Some stories, facts and quotations to help you

- *In the end, man destroyed the heaven that had been called earth. For the earth had been beautiful and happy until the destructive spirit of men moved upon it. This was the seventh day before the end.*

For man said, 'Let me have power in the earth,' and he saw that power seemed good, and he called those who sought power 'great leaders', and those who had sought to serve others and bring reconciliation 'weaklings, compromisers, appeasers'. And this was the sixth day before the end.

And man said, 'Let there be a division among all people, and divide the nations which are for me from the nations which are against me.' And this was the fifth day before the end.

And man said, 'Let us gather our resources in one place and create more instruments of power to defend ourselves; the radio to control men's minds, conscription to control men's bodies; uniforms and symbols of power to win men's souls.' And this was the fourth day before the end.

And man said, 'Let there be censorship to divide the propaganda from the truth.' And he made two great censorship bureaux to control the thoughts of men; one to tell only the truth he wishes known at home, and the other to tell only the truth that he wishes known abroad. And this was the third day before the end.

And man said, 'Let us create weapons which can kill vast numbers, even millions and hundreds of millions, at a distance.' And so he perfected germ warfare and deadly underwater arsenals, guided missiles, great fleets of war-planes and destructive power to the extent of tens of thousands of millions of tons of TNT. And it was the second day before the end.

And man said, 'Let us make God in our own image. Let us say God does as we do, thinks as we think, wills as we will, and kills as we kill.' So man found ways to kill with atomic power and dust, even those as yet unborn. And he said, 'This is necessary. There is no alternative. It is God's will.'

And on the last day, there was a great noise upon the face of the earth, and man and all his doings were no more, and the ravished earth rested on the seventh day.

Anon

• *Last week I wore new shoes to a wedding. Mistake! They gave me a blister and I limped to the reception. But this week some process I barely understand has got to work to heal the skin. The same is true of the earth. Forces that God has placed in it work slowly but endlessly to heal the world. Poisons get broken down to their harmless constituents in the sea and air. Trees convert the carbon dioxide that humans breathe out into the oxygen that we need. Here is God's plan for the planet, every part supporting some other part and every creature in its place. But what happens when humans invent chemicals so complex that the sea fights a losing battle to keep pace with the poisons poured into it (poisons such as those we use to varnish our nails or give toilet paper a pretty colour)? Or when humans pull down trees so fast that those left cannot cope with the vast quantities of harmful gas we release so that each of us can be driven around in our own little metal box?*
Peter Graystone

• *And he showed me more, a little thing, the size of a hazelnut, on the palm of my hand, rounded like a ball. I looked at it thoughtfully and wondered, 'What is this?' And the answer came, 'It is all that is made.' I marvelled that it continued to exist and did not suddenly disintegrate; it was so small. And again my mind supplied the answer, 'It exists both now and forever, because God loves it.' In short, everything owes its existence to the love of God.*
Julian of Norwich (Revelations of Divine Love, 1373)

• *Humans have often been part of God's healing process. Of hundreds of species that have become extinct in the wild over the last ten years, humans have reintroduced eighteen to their natural habitat through breeding in captivity. It's a desperately slow process, but it works. However, damage is not a slow process. It seemed that sea otters had been hunted to extinction for their pelts until a tiny colony was found in Alaska and helped, cub by cub, back into a substantial population. Then on Good Friday 1989 the Exxon Valdez spilled ten million gallons of oil into the sea and killed twelve thousand at a stroke.*

• *Despoiling the earth is a blasphemy, and not just an error of judgement, a mistake.*
Church of England Board of Social Responsibility

• *Only when the last tree has died and the last river has been poisoned and the last fish has been caught, will we realise that we cannot eat money.*
North American Cree Indian declaration

• *Christians alone know that this wonderful Earth which God has created for us doesn't belong to us: it belongs to Christ. At the end of time, when there will be a renewed and perfected heaven and earth, all the created order, which Christ won back to God through the cross, will be presented to him as his own. Then, as the earth returns to the one for whom it was created, we will be held accountable for what we have done with it. And will God forgive us? Of course he will! He forgives us again and again, as often as we ask. So I am not without hope, for even now it is not too late to turn to him, finding forgiveness and committing ourselves to change. But actions have consequences, even forgiven actions, and we have to live with the results of what we do to our planet. We must know this. Our children must know this. Our neighbours must know this. Our leaders must know this. In this generation time is not on our side. Let it be clear. This is the last ditch. This is where we turn and fight.*
Peter Graystone

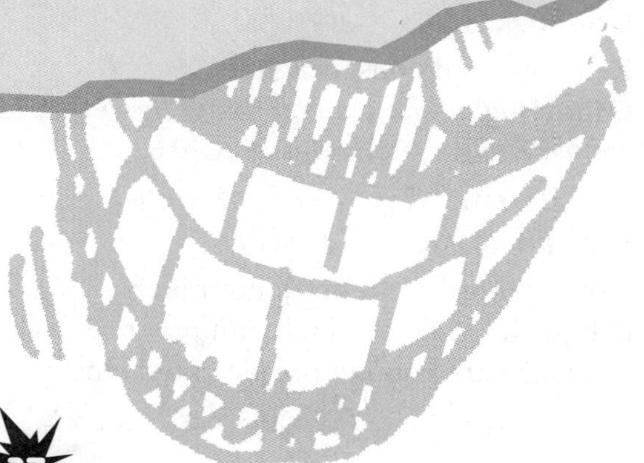

Issues concerned with... multi-faith and multi-cultural society

PART 1

SHOCK drama

How to create a successful assembly

CHARACTERS

- **Sir** (stereotypical male teacher, in a tweed jacket, leather patches at the elbows, corduroy trousers, maybe with a beard or glasses)
- **Rachel** (in school uniform)

PROPS

A book, with the title 'How to create a successful assembly' written clearly across the cover

Rachel is sitting on a table, feet dangling, reading the book. Sir stands gazing out through the audience, stroking his chin thoughtfully.

Rachel: Oh sir. *(Puts down book in disgust.)* Can't we just listen to Blur tracks or watch an Oasis video on the screen?

Sir: No we can't, Rachel. This assembly has got to have religious content.

Rachel: There are a few people in 9C who worship that Noel Gallagher ... do you think that counts? *(Sir shakes his head and rolls his eyes disapprovingly.)*

Rachel: No, I suppose not. Well, what do you think we should do?

Sir: I really don't know. What does it say in that book?

Rachel: Religious, religious, religious... *(Muttering as she scans through the contents page.)* Religious! Page 16.

Sir: Give it to me. *(Takes the book at the appropriate page and reads.)*

Sir: 'Sing hymns.' Well, that's not much help, is it? We'd need a hymn practice to make sure enough people could sing along, and even then we'd have to stick to ones we knew. I think 'All things bright and beautiful' is a bit much five times a week. *(Rips the page from the book.)*

Rachel: Why does it have to be hymns, sir? Couldn't we have a jazzed up chorus, something like 'Shine Jesus Shine'?

Sir: Whatever that is! I don't think it would be appropriate for a school assembly, do you?

Rachel: No sir! Only joking! But it would have been interesting to see if the headteacher raised his hands during the chorus. *(Straightens up and fixes an austere look at the audience, then changes her expression to a vacuous grin and raises an upturned hand as if in worship. Then returns to her normal pose.)*

Rachel: No, perhaps not. Well, what else does it say?

Sir: *(Flicking through book.)* 'Prayer'. There's something in here about the Lord's Prayer.

Rachel: That's no good, sir. What about Jubeda Khan? Her parents take her out of assembly if there's any Christian prayers, and she's not the only one.

Sir: *(Rips out another page.)* Mmm! Oh, here we are. *(Reads.)* 'No assembly should be without a rendition of the school hymn. The effects on morale through a sense of togetherness cannot be underestimated.' Mmm!

Rachel: Exactly, sir – mmm! We haven't got a school hymn, have we?

Sir: We used to have, I think. Don't know what it would be though. Perhaps it was 'The Journey of Life'.

Rachel: 'The Road to Nowhere' more like. No one would take it seriously … *(Sir rips out another page.)* Unless…

Sir: *(Hopefully.)* Yes? Unless what?

Rachel: Well, we could always adapt one of those ancient Take That singles…

Sir: *(Trying to interrupt her.)* Oh Rachel!

Rachel: They did some really good religious stuff … there was 'Pray'. *(Looks doubtful.)* And, er….

Sir: Rachel, let's try and keep this realistic, shall we?

Rachel: Yes, sir, 'Pray' was a good one though.

Sir: Mmm! Perhaps, but I can't really see it catching on amongst the senior staff, can you? *(Rips out another page.)* What about this? 'The Headmaster's Prayer'?

Rachel: Oh no, he'd only turn it into a lecture: 'Please God, help us do our best for the school and not drop litter or smoke behind the bike sheds.'
(She gets a disapproving teacher's look from Sir.)

Rachel: Well, he would! And anyway, what about Jubeda?

Sir: *(Rips out another page.)* What about a sermon?
(Rachel looks at him in disbelief. He shrugs his shoulders and makes another rip.)

Sir: Oh … oh really! This is getting impossible. *(Rips out more pages and flings down what remains of the book in disgust.)* That's it! I give up.
(Rachel is sorting through the torn pieces of paper that have been thrown down.)

Sir: That's the end of the book. I've run out of things to read. It's left us with nothing. *(Begins to leave.)* Nothing at all.
(He goes. Rachel holds up something she has unfolded from the paper. It is the shape of a cross. She recognises it, but can't think where from. She holds it up looking puzzled for a moment and then rises to follow Sir, holding the cross in front of her.)

Rachel: Sir? … Sir???

short sharp SHOCK

To be announced to the whole group as a dilemma

In 2005 the government pushed through a measure designed to reflect the increasingly multi-faith nature of British society. It radically changed what happened in the classroom. By an act of law every school now has to provide lesson time in every subject for every pupil with a teacher of his or her own faith. Muslims may, if they choose, study only with Muslims. Buddhists may, if they choose, study only with Buddhists. Or they can opt to have multi-faith lessons with people of all kinds of religious opinion or none, at which any reference to God is discouraged. Most of your Christian friends have joined the special class so that they can learn alongside other Christians and have their faith and morality respected.

For discussion in small groups:

Do you go with them or stay to study in a non-religious environment?

PART 2

bible SHOCK

For discussion in small groups

1. Read Genesis 5:1–2. Every human being on earth has been made in the image of God; we are all his children. The people in your group may have widely differing views, even if they are all of the same faith. Pray that during the discussion no one will forget that each of us is created by God, who loves a Christian as much as a Buddhist! And pray that God's love will be in you, taking away prejudice and fear.

2. Read Matthew 9:9–13. What do you think it was about Jesus' character which allowed him to enjoy the company of non-religious people so much, but still remain free from any sin or immorality?

3. Read verse 13 again. Jesus is saying here that there are greater qualities than strict religious observance. Can you name some valuable things that you have learnt from non-Christians which you could not have learnt from Christians? In what ways have you really experienced a Christian having a good influence in a non-Christian setting?

4. Read 1 Peter 2:9–12. These verses call us in some ways to be set apart from the non-Christian world, and in some ways to be completely involved in every part of the world. Since there are so many religions in the country now, sometimes there are situations in which people of different faiths are together when an act of worship is taking place. What would it be right for people of different faiths to do together in worship? When should Christians say, 'No, I can't do that because my faith is different'?

5. Some people asked Paul what made Christianity different from any other way of life. His answer is in Colossians 1:15–23. Read it now. It is full of complicated stuff. Have a go at writing a simpler answer for someone who asks: 'Why is your Christianity different from any other religion or way of life? Isn't everyone just looking at the same truth from a different angle?'

6. Throughout history some shameful things have been done by Christians to people of other faiths. What actions could you and your group take to avoid the prejudice and racism that have arisen from wrong attitudes toward people of other faiths?

SHOCK waves

Materials: Pens and paper.

Write an open letter, either to God or to the rest of the group, suggesting how relations with people from other races and faiths in the area could be improved, and listing some of the ideas that have emerged from your study of the Bible.

PART 3

SHOCK absorber

Prayers and acts of praise in seven contrasting styles from which to choose

A selection of songs and hymns:

- All heaven declares, *Songs of Fellowship* (4)
- And he shall reign, *Songs of Fellowship* (5)
- Jesus, Jesus, holy and anointed One, *Songs of Fellowship* (revised edition)
- Meekness and majesty, *Songs of Fellowship* (4), *Mission Praise* (2)
- We believe in God the Father, *Songs of Fellowship* (4), *Mission Praise* (2)
- When I survey the wondrous cross, *Songs of Fellowship* (H), *Mission Praise* (1)
- You laid aside Your majesty, *Songs of Fellowship* (3), *Mission Praise* (2)

Using the Shock Waves responses

Take time to allow each group to read out their letters, either as a prayer to God or as an address to the rest of the groups in God's presence. While the letters are being read, no one else is allowed to interrupt or challenge. However, after there has been a chance for reflection, the group may talk and pray together to decide what they can support practically.

Led prayer

Father, thank you for the diversity of culture.
When we meet what we are not used to, keep fear far from us.
Give us courage to seek out encounters with people from unfamiliar cultures:
May your humility make us open to learn from them;
May your love make us eager to share with them;
And in your grace, may all who seek you, find you.
Amen.

Responsive prayer

For the richness of all your creation,
God of all, we praise you.

For snoozes in the sun and sprints in the rain,
God of all, we praise you.

For the first snow-drop of spring and the first goal of the season,
God of all, we praise you.

For films that get us thinking and videos that let us laugh,
God of all, we praise you.

For meeting new people at parties and long talks with a best friend,
God of all, we praise you.

For big, ugly centre-backs and little tricksy wingers,
God of all, we praise you.

For work finished in the small hours and lie-ins until the afternoon,
God of all, we praise you.

For lippy kids and wise old aunties,
God of all, we praise you.

For big slap-up meals and quick snacks at break time,
God of all, we praise you.

For the British weather,
God of all, we praise you.

For relaxing with what we like and being challenged by what we're not sure of,
God of all, we praise you.

For the security of belonging and the freshness of what we've never seen before,
God of all, we praise you. Amen.

Open prayer

Suggest that those present get into whatever size group they feel comfortable with and spend a few minutes remembering sections in society whose members are most subject to prejudice and discrimination. They may want to tell their group a name and some circumstances so that they can then pray for specific people and circumstances.

Silent reflection

Read Revelation 7:9–10 aloud to the whole group. Invite the group to shut their eyes and imagine the great multitude from every nation, tribe, people and language worshipping together. Imagine, for example, a Nigerian worshipping alongside an Eskimo, a Chinese shaking hands with a Russian, a Croat with a Serb, a Hutu and a Tutsi, nationalists and loyalists running through the streets of Ireland to greet each other. Close the meditation by going on to read Revelation 7:11–12.

Creative prayer

Give each person a sticky label and a pencil. Suggest that everyone writes the name of someone known to them from another faith – it could be someone they have met or someone of whom they are aware through the media – along with a symbol that represents what each would like to pray for the person they have named. Place a card cross on the floor in the middle of the group and allow time for each person to come forward and place their label on the card. While this is happening, the song 'Wherever God shines his light', from the album *Avalon Sunset* by Van Morrison, could be played. When everyone who wants to has contributed and has read the contributions of others, display the cross on a wall and close the prayer by reading Romans 16:25–27.

talking SHOCK

Outline of a talk

- Christians believe that there are some things everybody in the world shares.
- Everyone has been made different, but all are equal.
- Every human has been made in the image of God (Genesis 5:1).
- We share the need to worship God – and the same tendency to hide from him.
- We all have the same ability to see his work in nature (Romans 1:20).
- And everyone, Christian or not, is equally loved by God.

The New Testament pleads with Christians not to cut themselves off from the world outside the church – but it also instructs them to live in a way which distinctively avoids all that is not good about the world outside (Romans 12:1–2).

God can use anyone to do his will – not just Christians. When the Jews were in exile in Babylon (eighty dreadful years after a defeat in battle), the person God chose to rescue them was from a completely alien religion. God's regard for King Cyrus of Persia is so high that he uses the same language for him that is later used of Jesus – he calls him anointed (Isaiah 45:1). It could hardly be clearer that God intends his people to benefit from other cultures.

In the New Testament too, Paul recognised God's work happening within other religions and cultures. In a sermon he gave in Athens he quoted pagan poets, saying that they had got things right about God. He didn't say that every other religion has it all wrong; instead, he said that there was much, much more to be discovered, and invited the people to consider the claims of Jesus (Acts 17:16–34).

As Christians we have a call to bring others to Jesus, but Christians have done terrible damage in the past. Our first priorities when talking to people from other religions or cultures should be to listen, to learn, and to understand. Even Jesus found himself learning from people of other faiths (Matthew 8:10). He found positive things to say about them which he could not find in those of his own religion (Matthew 8:11–12).

We need to be careful never to say anything that makes Jesus out to be less than our unique God, but never to be judgmental or bulldoze someone else's opinion. We probably need to step back from the kind of worship which makes Jesus only one of many people to whom we could pray. However, never in any circumstances be racist or self-satisfied in any approach to those who do not share our beliefs – the image of God is in them, and if we cannot see it, it is we who are blind.

Some stories, facts and quotations to help you

- *I was talking to a West Indian student in our college dining room. With a broad Birmingham accent she told me that she had been born in this country and had never even visited Jamaica, where her forefathers originally came from. As we talked further, I realised that her family had come to Britain before mine! This came as quite a shock to me. Because I am white and English, people do not think of me as an immigrant, whereas she is always being taken for an immigrant because she has a deep black skin and curly West Indian hair. But she is, in fact, as much a native of this country as I am. Today you don't have to be white to be British, though many white people have difficulty accepting it.*

Martin Goldsmith and Rosemary Harley (Who is my Neighbour?, Scripture Union)

- *My karma has just run over my dogma.*

Graffiti

- *Only a small number of the more recent newcomers to Britain are Christians. It is true that many West Indians, increasing numbers of Chinese and some Jews, Indians and Pakistanis are Christian, but most are not. In our resident British population we now have over 1,000,000 Muslims (more than all the Methodists and Baptists put together), more than 300,000 non-Christian Jews, and about 300,000 Sikhs as well as many Hindus and Buddhists. The mosque, temple and synagogue form part of the mosaic of British life. Today you don't have to be even nominally Christian to be British.*

Martin Goldsmith and Rosemary Harley

A faith is something you die for; a doctrine is something you kill for – there is all the difference in the world.

Tony Benn

- *In Germany, the Nazis came for the communists, and I didn't speak up, because I was not a Communist. Then they came for the Jews, and I didn't speak up, because I was not a Jew … Then they came for the Catholics, and I was a Protestant, so I didn't speak up. Then they came for me … By that time there was no one to speak up for anyone.*

Martin Niemoller

- *I have a dream that one day on the red hills of Georgia the sons of former slaves and the sons of former slave-owners will be able to sit down together at the table of brotherhood. I have a dream that one day even the state of Mississippi, a state sweltering with the heat of injustice … and oppression, will be transformed into an oasis of freedom and justice. I have a dream that my four children will one day live in a nation where they will be judged not by the colour of their skin but by the content of their characters. I have a dream that one day in Alabama, with its vicious racists … little black boys and black girls will be able to join hands with little white boys and white girls as sisters and brothers … With this faith we will be able to transform the jangling discords of our nation into a beautiful symphony of brotherhood. With this faith we will be able to work together to stand up for freedom together, knowing that we will be free one day.*

Martin Luther King Jr

- *I define integration not as a flattening process of assimilation, but as equal opportunity accompanied by cultural diversity in an atmosphere of mutual tolerance.*

Roy Jenkins

- *The Jews and Arabs should sit down and settle their differences like good Christians.*

Warren Austin (US diplomat)

- *God has no religion … We would all be Christians if it were not for the Christians.*

Mahatma Gandhi

- *Our society has taken Jesus and recreated him in our own cultural image. When I hear Jesus being proclaimed from the television stations across our country, from pulpits hither and yon, he comes across not as the biblical Jesus, but as a white, Anglo-Saxon, Protestant Republican. God created us in his image, but we have decided to return the favour and create a God who is in our image.*

Tony Campolo

6 Issues concerned with... entertainment

PART 1

SHOCK drama

World theatre

CHARACTERS
- **Cherub**
- **Seraph**
- **Off-stage voice**

PROPS
Two chairs, popcorn, a programme, dry ice (optional).

One of the angels is sitting waiting, as if in a theatre or cinema, for the other to arrive and the performance to begin. Dry ice would give the impression of cloud.

Cherub: *(To his friend off-stage.)* You're going to miss it. Come on! Quickly!

Seraph: *(Enters and sits down.)* Sorry! I was just buying these.

Cherub: What are they?

Seraph: I got you a programme. *(Gives it to the cherub.)*

Cherub: Oh thanks!

Seraph: And this is popcorn.

Cherub: Popcorn! That isn't invented for several million years.

Seraph: It's a prototype. They're doing a survey of flavours so that they're ready when the time comes. There's three and they're trying to narrow it down to two.

Cherub: So what are the flavours?

Seraph: There's salt, sugar, or this.

Cherub: *(Tries some.)* Cabbage!

Seraph: Do you think it will catch on?

Cherub: It'll take a lot of advertising! Hey, look! The lights are coming up!

Seraph: I've been looking forward to this. Who's the director?

Cherub: *(Looks at the programme.)* It's one of God's productions.

Seraph: Brilliant! It's going to be perfect.

Cherub: Shh! It's beginning!

Seraph: *(Whispers.)* How long does it last?

Cherub: Six days.

Seraph: Is that all?

Cherub: We're only seeing the short version. The full-length version is forty billion years. It's because ... uuuh! ... *(Struck speechless at the beauty of the sight.)*

Seraph: Wow! Amazing! Amazing! Lights, colours, flashes in the sky! Vast spectra of incandescent illumination. Darkness and light in ever-changing, ever-constant magnificence. It's scarcely believable! What do you think?

Cherub: Uuuh!

Seraph: Exactly! Praise the Creator God. Alleluia! Alleluia!

Cherub: *(Nods!)* Uuuh!

Seraph: The heavens and the earth. Deep waters and lofty lands. Mountains and valleys. Countless millions of planets whirling effortlessly round a billion suns. Constellations of luminous stars, nebulae glittering across incandescent galaxies. Have you ever seen anything so beautiful?

Cherub: *(Points.)* Uuu-uuh!

Seraph: What is it? What can you see?

Cherub: Thhh-thhh!

Seraph: All I can see is a tiny little green thing! Is that what you're looking at?

Cherub: Uuuh-thhh!

Seraph: Obviously it is! A pretty little green planet! Any idea what it's called?

Cherub: Uuuh-thhh!

Seraph: Earth! Well, well! Lovely name!

Cherub: *(Speaking with difficulty.)* It's the chosen one!

Seraph: Chosen?

Cherub: For the humans.

Seraph: Oh, for the human beings! Of course! Well, isn't that typical of God. He hasn't chosen the biggest planet or the brightest or the fastest. Earth! What a great home that is going to be for the finest things in God's creation!

Cherub: Finest! Hmm!

Seraph: Shall I tell you what impresses me most? Our wonderful Creator God has decided to make human beings in his image. They're going to be creative, just like him. They're going to look at the world God has made and be amazed by its beauty and its grace. And they're going to use the creativity God has put inside them to shape it and arrange it and order it so that their fellow humans are moved and exhilarated and filled to overflowing with enjoyment. Sensational! What an opportunity! What would you give to be human?

Cherub: Well now, that's a good question!

Seraph: *(Not really listening.)* There's going to be music, there's going to be entertainment, there's going to be art which thrills the soul. And every part of it giving glory to the Creator himself.

Cherub: Glory! Hmm!

Seraph: All these wonderful things created for human beings to make their lives rich. I think it's ... I think it's ...

Cherub: What's the matter?

Seraph: I've just had an awful thought.

Cherub: You too?

Seraph: What if ... what if one of the humans starts to use his creativity for selfish reasons instead of ones which honour God?

Cherub: Or her!

Seraph: The results could be terrible!

Cherub: *(Grins.)* Terrible!

Seraph: It might end up with art being reduced to pornography. Sick pornography! Entertainment might end up just as propaganda. Can you imagine the manipulation that could take place? It could all turn into cheap salesmanship. Just a chance to make money out of people's worst instincts. Surely something so full of glorious potential could never stoop so low as that? Do you think it could happen?

Cherub: I'm thinking it right now! *(Pause, while they both look forward, the cherub with dawning mischief, the seraph with growing despondency.)*

Voice: All angels on stage please. All angels to get ready.

Seraph: Oh! What's happening?

Cherub: It's the interval.

Seraph: Oh my word! We must go. It's our part in a moment. *(Rising.)* I'm dancing the solo in the celestial ballet to the music of the spheres. I don't dare be late.

Voice: This is your last call. All angels ready please.

Seraph: I'm on my way. *(Exits.)*

Cherub: Yes, I'll be on my way in a moment too.

Seraph: *(Reappears to get the cherub.)* Come on, Satan, we'll be late.

Cherub: Shortly, Gabriel! Just give me time to think!

short sharp SHOCK

To be announced to the whole group as a dilemma

There was a change in cinema rules in 2006. Public outcry over increasing violence led to a tightening-up of what was acceptable in each category of film. The new 18 certificate was given to films which previously would have got an 15 certificate, and so on. The cinema industry fought back, arguing that they would be ruined financially by the new restrictions, and in the end there was a compromise – the certificates 12, 15 and 18 (and the new one – 21) became merely advisory instead of compulsory. There was some debate among Christians as to whether they should treat the recommendations as absolute rules, or whether they should take advantage of the new freedoms.

For discussion in small groups:

As a Christian, would you see a 21 film before you reached that age under these new laws?

PART 2

bible SHOCK

For discussion in small groups

❶ Read Exodus 35:30 – 36:1. This is a discussion about something that is very important to everyone's life, so pray that God will allow your group to change as a result of the conversation and enjoy TV, music, cinema and so on, even more than before.

❷ Read verse 31 again. This says that it is the Holy Spirit alone who enables people to be creative or artistic. In the passage it applies to decoration – making the church-tent where the Israelites worshipped (the tabernacle) a spectacular contrast to the dull desert. And of course, if humans are made in the image of the Creator God, then they are naturally creative (Genesis 1:27). Does this apply to making films and chart-songs as much as making jewellery and embroidery? Can you think of any modern art or entertainment that it doesn't apply to?

❸ If creativity is a gift of the Holy Spirit in every human, why is so much art and entertainment naff? Does 36:1 give any suggestions?

❹ Read Philippians 4:4–8. Can you think of any circumstances in which God would want us to 'guard our hearts and minds' (verse 7) against certain types of entertainment? Can you think of specific examples to which Christians might say, 'No, I won't see or hear that?' Is there anything to which Christians should say, 'No, I won't see that, and nobody else ought to see it either.'

❺ Read verse 8 again. Can you think of a specific film, TV, music, theatre, picture, etc, which seems to fit each category on the checklist? *Reservoir Dogs* was a very violent 1992 film about greed, loyalty, honesty and sin. In the cinema it had an 18 certificate, but the censors refused to allow it to be released on video. It certainly wasn't lovely, but it was true and excellently made. Does that make it good or bad for Christians to see? What about for Christians under 18 to see?

SHOCK waves

Materials: Various, to give as much flexibility as possible to the groups. Items could include large pieces of card, pencils and paper, paint and brushes, spray-paint, scissors, felt markers, pieces of material, a typewriter, musical instruments, a cassette recorder, a variety of taped music, face paints, 'clown' costumes, Plasticine or modelling clay, a camcorder, a Polaroid camera, an overhead projector and pens, sewing materials.

Working in small groups or individually, decide on a way of expressing one of the things you have talked about concerning the arts and entertainment during this discussion. The way it is presented must involve the creativity of the group and represent one of the styles of entertainment that have been mentioned. For example, members of the group could write a song, devise a drama or mime, paint a picture, make a sculpture or collage, create a banner, make a short film on video, record a radio broadcast or documentary, choreograph a dance, compile a photo-montage, write a poem, psalm or short story, or conceive performance art.

PART 3

SHOCK absorber

Prayers and acts of praise in seven contrasting styles from which to choose

A selection of songs and hymns:

- Come let us sing, *Songs of Fellowship* (4)
- God is good, *Songs of Fellowship* (3), *Mission Praise* (2)
- Jesus put this song into our hearts, *Songs of Fellowship* (4), *Mission Praise* (2)
- Let us praise His name with dancing, *Songs of Fellowship* (4)
- Praise Him on the trumpet, *Songs of Fellowship* (2), *Mission Praise* (2)
- Praise the Lord, praise God, *Songs of Fellowship* (2), *Mission Praise* (2)
- Shout for joy to the Lord all the earth, *Songs of Fellowship* (3)
- Sing to God, *Mission Praise* (2) and recent hymn books

Using the Shock Waves responses

Give everyone who has devised a response to what they have discovered in the Bible a chance to perform, describe, read, display or broadcast it. Try to create an atmosphere in which the whole group accepts and gives encouragement for each contribution as an act of worship.

Led prayer

May none of God's wonderful works keep silence, night or morning;
Bright stars, high mountains, the depths of the seas, sources of rushing rivers:
May all these break into song as we sing to Father, Son and Holy Spirit.
May all the angels in the heavens reply:
Amen, amen, amen.
Power, praise, honour, eternal glory to Jesus, the risen giver of grace,
Amen, amen, amen.

Anon (third century)

Responsive prayer

Based on words and images from Jeremiah 10:12–16:

Who made the earth by his power?
The Lord Almighty is his name.

Who by his wisdom created the world?
The Lord Almighty is his name.

Who stretched out the heavens above?
The Lord Almighty is his name.

Who commands thunder to roar in the sky?
The Lord Almighty is his name.

Who makes lightning flash in the rain?
The Lord Almighty is his name.

Whose are the clouds and the winds and the waters?
The Lord Almighty is his name.

Singers and dancers, know your Creator,
The Lord Almighty is his name.

Craftsmen and goldsmiths, know your Creator,
The Lord Almighty is his name.

Writers and poets, know your Creator,
The Lord Almighty is his name.

Who takes joy in his creative people?
The Lord Almighty is his name.

Open prayer

Either in small groups or as one large group, offer God prayers of thanksgiving for pieces of art or entertainment that are particularly inspiring or enjoyable. These could be specific singers, films, books, plays, types of music, and so on.

Silent reflection

In a time of silence, invite everyone to bring to mind various pieces of art or entertainment that they have experienced recently. In the silence, invite them to dwell on the piece, and reflect on what they have learnt through experiencing it – for good or ill. As they reflect, they may find their minds turning to God with thanks, concern, repentance, or a determination to change either themselves or the world. After an explanation of what will happen, introduce the meditation by inviting the group to bring to mind a film or play … a song or piece of music …, a television programme … a visual image … (optionally) something you have read … Conclude this time with these lines by Dag Hammarskjold:

You take the pen – and the lines dance.
You take the flute – and the notes shimmer.
You take the brush – and the colours sing.
So all things have meaning and beauty in that space beyond time where you are.
How, then, can I hold anything back from you?

Creative prayer

Give everyone a square of paper, using as many different colours as possible. (For the ideal size, trim the tops off pieces of A4 paper to make them square – craft shops sell coloured paper already cut to these dimensions.) Give the following instructions, demonstrating them as you speak:

1 Fold the paper in half from left to right so that you make a rectangle.
2 Fold it from top to bottom so that it is square again.
3 Fold along the diagonal so that you make a triangle.
4 Tear out little pieces from all round the edges of the triangle – a dozen, or as many as you can, some big, some small.
5 Open it out and look at the attractive symmetrical piece of 'art' that you have made.
6 Using Blu-tack, attach everybody's design to a wall so that a large quilt-like pattern is formed.

Follow this with a prayer:

Creator God, who saw everything you made to be good, accept as our offering this work of art. In its many colours, may it praise you for your vivid goodness. In its symmetry may it praise you for the order and control you have placed upon your world. In the co-operation that went into making it may it praise you for the trust you have placed in us. In its beauty may it praise you for your radiant splendour. Magnificent Creator, may you take joy in our work of praise. Amen.

talking SHOCK

Outline of a talk

There is nothing bad about true creativity – it is good. God the Creator made us in his own image, so his intention has always been that we should be creative people. The spirit which drives people to make and listen to music, to create TV and to want to be entertained by TV, is the Holy Spirit. It was so for the artists of the Bible (Exodus 35:30–31), and God is the source of all song and dance, whether or not people realise it (Psalm 87:7).

But like everything else, its basic goodness can be hijacked. That is why Christians are more dismayed than anyone else when art is debauched into pornography, hijacked into propaganda or used to titillate people's worst instincts.

Jesus never went to a multiplex, so it is no good looking for references to cinema in the Bible! However, there is a lot in the Bible about dance, which was as an important form of entertainment then as it is now. Is dance good or bad? Both! When the Hebrews crossed the Red Sea, God was clearly delighted with the way they used dance to celebrate (Exodus 15:19–20). But they were quite capable of abusing dance and art in entertainment, even at a religious event (Exodus 32:5–6,19). The psalms affirm many times God's delight in dance (Psalm 150:4). But that didn't stop Herodias realising that dance is so powerful that it can turn people's heads – she persuaded her daughter to dance so alluringly that the king agreed to give her what she wanted – the death of Jesus' cousin John (Matthew 14:6–10).

Look below the surface of entertainment to see whether it has godly values at its heart (Philippians 4:8). That way you can distinguish between what brings out the best in you, and what you are being persuaded to enjoy by the hype. Strike back against any kind of entertainment that works against the good God intended, by making, listening to, looking at and thanking God for as much honourable music and art as you can!

As a Christian, wherever you go, you take Jesus with you. When you decide to take Jesus to an entertainment, give him a good time!

Some stories, facts and quotations to help you

- *I think music is spiritual. Singing, playing an instrument is spiritual. It's coming from a spiritual world.*

  Van Morrison

- *If God hadn't given me a song to sing, I wouldn't have a song to sing.*

  Bob Marley

- *I believe in God and respect God. Before we go on stage we all gather together and pray. We give thanks for our safety, we ask for the blessing of the audience, that everybody is healthy and well, and we ask for the strength and energy to go out and do what we do.*

  M C Hammer

- *Mad Christians walk around outside my gigs with placards saying Billy Idol is the next Anti-Christ, which is stupid because my lyrics support love and gorgeousness.*

  Billy Idol

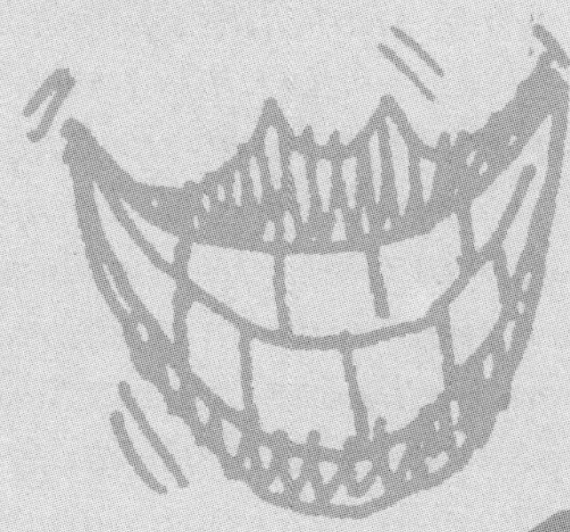

• *A reporter from* The Independent *visited Albania shortly after the fall of communism there:*
A young woman told me that during the years when religion was banned, this church was used as a school gym.
'If a girl was naughty or inattentive, she was punished by having to stay on afterwards to paint over the church murals … I was born in 1967, the year they abolished religion, but I was secretly baptised at the age of two. My grandmother taught me the liturgy and on Easter Day she secretly painted some eggs red. That may sound childish, but to me it was very beautiful and wonderful…'
Socialist art, with its strident, boastful exaltation of power, is empty, indeed repulsive. The architecture is uniformly depressing and hideous. Even the mass-produced clothes are coloured the drabbest of browns and greys. The Albanians have lived with no more spiritual, emotional or artistic nourishment than could be found in the speeches of Enver Hoxha, or art and literature of which he approved. Things which we take for granted, such as a fine mediaeval church, a hymn … the words of the twenty-third psalm, or even an egg painted red for a little girl's Easter present, seem to Albanians beautiful and wonderful.

• *Two recent photographs illustrate how we can look behind potentially shocking images to see whether we are being asked to glorify the Creator or open ourselves to the manipulation of a creator. When Madonna spreads her naked legs in front of a crucifix and gives her photograph a title that mixes up religious words with four-letter words, she isn't saying anything about the power of God – in fact she is expressing her own power to titillate and make money. However, although Andres Serrano's photograph of a plastic crucifix dropped into urine so outraged American senator Jesse Helms that he tore it up in the Senate House in Washington, it is a technically excellent image which tells of the photographer's realisation of the shocking truth that the holy God left the perfection of Heaven and came to earth as Jesus to be baptised into all sordid human reality. If we lose track of what it cost God to do that on our behalf, what kind of shock does it take to bring us back to wonder that he freely chose it? Perhaps the kind of truth that art and entertainment can expose even when asking us to see something ugly – a truth and purity certainly not shared by the cheap plastic crucifix, mass-produced for gain in a godless country.*
Peter Graystone

• *We need to distinguish between what is pretty and what is good. It is possible to imagine a worship tape which is pretty to listen to, but so shoddily put together or superficial or cringe-making that it cheapens God rather than honou him. It is much more difficult to define goodness in music. House of Pain are Irish-American rappers who use their coarse discords to devalue women's rights and promote the sense that violence against homosexuals is acceptable:*
'I'll serve your ass like John McEnroe
If your girl steps up I'm smacking the ho'…
I'll snatch you by the ear, smack you up like a queer
Take a puff of my blunt and then sip my beer.'
Billy Bragg is an Essex rock singer whose coarse, scraped, missed notes are not even slightly more lyrical, but whose songs reflect the pain of infidelity, poverty and restlessness:
'In public he's such a man
He's punching at the walls with his bare and bloody hands
He's screaming and shouting and acting crazy
But at home he sits alone and cries like a baby…
You said this would happen and you were not wrong
I've fallen in love with a little time bomb.'
Which is pretty? Which is honourable?

• *Our society makes us out of touch with ourselves. The churches are finished; we don't have a pow-wow, a place to be emotional. The closest we have to that is a really great concert. There's an identification: the person on stage is supposed to express how they feel and the audience get it, they can weep, dance, go berserk, whatever they like. I think that's important. Singers are shamanistic in a funny sort of way.*
Annie Lennox

• *All I've got is a red guitar, three chords and the truth – the rest is up to you.*
Bono

7 Issues concerned with... alcohol and drugs

PART 1

SHOCK drama

Jingle all the way

CHARACTERS

- **Man** (getting progressively more and more drunk)
- **Woman**
- **Voice** (unseen, audible to the man and the audience, but not to the woman)
- **Advert** (unseen, and speaking only in advertising jingles)
- There are other characters, to whom the man and woman talk, but we cannot see them

PROPS

Hip flask (or miniature bottle)
Two beer cans

The man swaggers on. He is followed by a young woman. He hands her his can, reaches into his back pocket and gets out a hip flask (or bottle). He sucks on his teeth as he swallows and looks around. He puts the flask back and goes to take back the can.

Woman: Take it easy, love.
(The man takes the can with a stare, then hears the voice. He can't work out where it is coming from or why the woman can't hear it.)

Voice: Are you having fun?
(The man wheels round to face the audience as if to answer the voice. He raises his can with a gesture of raucous assurance. He goes to take another mouthful, but realises that the can is empty. He gestures for the woman to go and find another drink.)

Advert: Seek out the lager of Lamot.

Woman: *(Hands the man another can.)* Something tells me it will be me driving home tonight.
(She walks to the side, miming conversation with invisible people. The man turns round to hold the can up in triumph.)

Voice: So, are you going to meet someone special tonight?
(The man raises his drink in hopeful assent and, as he does so, he catches sight of someone entering the room. His eyes follow her eagerly as the imaginary figure gets closer and closer. He lets a stupid grin spread across his face as she appears to pass by, and he closes his eyes to drink in her perfume. Meanwhile, the woman glances over her shoulder, concerned at what is going on.)

Advert: By 'eck, you smell gorgeous tonight, petal.
(The man nods in eager agreement.)

Voice: *(Pause.)* Well, aren't you going to speak to her?
(The man looks out towards the audience and then wistfully towards where the imaginary girl has gone. He gulps some drink. The woman has been glancing round at him over her shoulder. She moves round so as to get a better view of what he is doing.)

Voice: Oh well, perhaps you're not being interesting enough. You should do something to impress.
(Man looks doubtful and takes another drink.)

Advert: Heineken refreshes the parts other beers cannot reach.
(The man listens doubtfully, but begins to move over to where we imagine the girl is standing. In mime, he begins to talk to her – nervously, then more confidently.)

Voice: Time to do something to impress.

Man: *(To the imaginary girl, pointing to the woman.)* Who her? Oh no! I'm my own, man. No one tells *me* what to do!

Woman: *(To an imaginary friend, pointing to the man.)* Who him? He's not himself half the time. He's always got so much to prove.

Man: *(To the imaginary girl.)* Yeah, I know my own mind. If I want something I usually get it.

Woman: *(To the imaginary friend.)* I'm not sure he can think straight after he's had a few beers.

Voice: Things are really going to plan now.

Advert: I bet he drinks Carling Black Label. *(The man nods towards the voice with a wink.)*

Voice: This is going better than you could have imagined.

Advert: When it calls for the best it calls for a Holsten Export.
(The man nods again and gives a thumbs-up sign, pleased with himself.)

Man: So ... do you come here often?

Woman: Often as not he's got a drink in his hand.

Voice: You could keep this up forever.

Advert: Any time, any place, anywhere.

Man: *(To girl.)* I'm not doing anything later on tonight, do you fancy ... *(But the girl is obviously walking away.)* Hey, wait a minute ... Where are you going?

Advert: Don't you just hate it when that happens.

Woman: *(To friend.)* And when I can't stand it any longer, there's only one thing to do. *(She walks over to the man, swings him round and slaps his face. She walks off, trying to keep her dignity.)*

Man: What did I do? What did I do?

Voice: Mmm, very clever!

Advert: Pure genius.
(The man looks decidedly queasy.)

Voice: Oh well, another drink and all this will seem like paradise.
(The man is about to throw up. He staggers to lean against the wall, his back to the audience.)

Advert: If ... you're drinking Bacardi.
(The man is violently sick.)

short sharp SHOCK

To be announced to the whole group as a dilemma

In 2007, a famous Stout brewery launched their new product 'Black-and-White'. This was a sweet, non-alcoholic drink for children with the distinctive black and white appearance that draught stout has always had. The brewery never attempted to disguise that their aim was to make children identify with the black and white appearance so that in later life they would become committed drinkers of the real alcoholic version. Ten-year-old boys love it because it makes them feel sophisticated when they drink it. Anti-drug agencies are appalled at something so likely to encourage alcoholism in later life. There is a boycott of this particular brewery's products.

For discussion in small groups:

Will you join the boycott?

ART 2

bible SHOCK

For discussion in small groups

❶ Read Matthew 9:14–15 and 11:16–19. As a result of what you talk about today, some people may want to make changes to their lifestyle. Pray that God will show you what decisions are wise.

❷ John the Baptist encouraged a lifestyle that totally avoided luxurious enjoyment – for instance, alcohol or rich food. Jesus came and was not afraid to mix with those who were enjoying themselves to the full at parties and feasts. Read 11:18–19 again. Who does Jesus say got it right?

❸ List the advantages for today's Christians of choosing a lifestyle completely free of alcohol, tobacco and other drugs (like John). Now list the advantages of moderate drinking and partying (of which Jesus was accused). What does Jesus mean in 11:19 when he says that 'wisdom is proved right by her actions'?

❹ Read Proverbs 23:29–35. Where does it say here that alcohol abuse is a threat to: (a) health, (b) judgment, (c) emotional stability, (d) self-control, (e) other people's well-being?

❺ When the writer of Proverbs was alive, wine was a medicine, a household drink, and a recreational drug. If he was alive today, he would probably list other substances as well as wine. What do you think he would have included? Make a list.

When there are a dozen or more on the list, divide them into three groups:

a those which Christians should categorically avoid for personal pleasure,
b those which Christians need to find a moderate way of enjoying but not abusing,
c those which don't seem to involve a moral decision, just a matter of taste.

When the grouping is complete, look at each group and see whether you can back up your decisions biblically or whether they are just personal common sense – or is there no difference?

SHOCK waves

Materials: Pieces of A4 coloured paper, scissors, felt markers, pens.

Working in small groups and using any of the materials provided, make a flyer advertising a party. On the advert, make it clear what the boundaries of the event are as far as various kinds of drug are concerned. Try to express through the content and style of your flyer the qualities you would want your party to have. Include as part of it some of the thoughts that have come out of your discussion of the Bible – either things that all the group are agreed on, or dilemmas about which you cannot agree.

PART 3

SHOCK absorber

Prayers and acts of praise in seven contrasting styles from which to choose

A selection of songs and hymns:

- I give You all the honour, *Songs of Fellowship* (3), *Mission Praise* (2)
- I love you, Lord, and I lift my voice, *Songs of Fellowship* (1), *Mission Praise* (1)
- Reign in me, *Songs of Fellowship* (4), *Mission Praise* (2)
- Rejoice! Rejoice! Christ is in you, *Songs of Fellowship* (3), *Mission Praise* (2)
- Spirit of the living God, *Songs of Fellowship* (4), *Mission Praise* (1)
- You are the rock, *Songs of Fellowship* (4)
- You did not wait for me, *Songs of Fellowship* (4)

Using the Shock Waves responses

The flyers should be displayed around the walls. Ask the group to get up and walk round the room in silence. They should pause in front of each one to reflect on what the group who created it were trying to communicate. They should use that as the basis of their own silent prayer, thanksgiving or promise-making to God. After some time (the length depending on how many flyers there are for the group to examine) play some quiet music, which is the sign for the participants to retake their seats.

Led prayer

Father,
Develop in us the mind of Christ that we might be truly free to make our own decisions,
Give us the vision of Christ that we may see others as you see them,
Grant us the security of Christ that our actions may be motivated by a desire to give and not a need for approval,
For the sake of life in all its fullness. Amen.

Responsive prayer

Forgive us, Father, when we lose patience with you and look for quicker solutions to our needs;
Giver of all life,
We hope and trust in you.

Thank you, Father, that we can rely on you for everything – you love us and know exactly what we need;
Giver of all life,
We hope and trust in you.

Forgive us, Father, for the dependencies we have built up that take no account of you;
Giver of all life,
We hope and trust in you.

Thank you, Father, that you want the best for us and can give us freedom where we have made ourselves prisoners;
Giver of all life,
We hope and trust in you.

Forgive us, Father, for the people around us who have heard nothing of you and look elsewhere for the things they need;
Giver of all life,
We hope and trust in you.

Thank you, Father, that you care for all and give us opportunities to tell others you are there;
Giver of all life,
We hope and trust in you.

Open prayer

Invite the group to spend a few minutes thinking of all that can be positive about drug use, making it clear that all kinds of drugs are included – aspirin, tea, coffee, alcohol, tobacco, soft drugs, Category A drugs. (Their thoughts might include medicinal purposes, taste, common identity with friends, relaxation, relief of pain.) Invite the group to turn their thoughts into prayers by calling out words or phrases as an expression of thanks for the positive side of drugs and their benefits. To bring the time of prayer to a close, the leader should say:

Lord God, make us wise as people, as a group, as a society. Amen.

Go on to invite consideration of all that is negative in drug use (perhaps including addiction, organised crime, breakdown of relationships, ill-health, loss of reality, paranoia, loss of self-esteem). Turn these into prayer as well, in single words and phrases. Close by saying:

Lord God, make us safe as people, as a group, as a society. Amen.

Silent reflection

Invite the group to shut their eyes and think of an occasion in their own experience which has involved drugs of any kind being used positively (medically, enhancing the joy of a social occasion, building friendship, etc). During a silence, they should thank God for the people who were involved, for the results of their experience, and for their own part in it. Then suggest they focus on one occasion at which they were present when drugs were used in a negative way (a way which gave discomfort to others, a time when misery was evidently the cause or the result of the drugs, an incident that scared them). Again they should remember in silence those who were involved, asking for help, for forgiveness, for healing – for themselves or for others. Thirdly, invite them to introduce the people they have been thinking of in both situations to Jesus. Suggest that they consider how Jesus would want to meet the needs that led to drugs being used – imagine him speaking to each person, consider what he is saying and doing. Close the time by reading Ephesians 3:16–19.

Creative prayer

Place on a table some objects which symbolically represent different kinds of drug which have been discussed. They should be symbols, not the substances themselves (eg, an empty wine bottle, not a full one). The objects could include a beer can, a spirits bottle, a cigarette packet, a coffee jar, a square of blotting paper, a pill bottle, a piece of foil, a syringe, etc. Provide pencils, paper, scissors, candles, flowers, ribbons, leaves, modelling materials, or anything else that could be used creatively. Invite the group, while some music is playing, to send a private message to God which is concerned with one of those symbols. It could be a letter, a particular person's name, a drawing, an action, and so on. They should place their offering or prayer in front of whichever of the symbols it seems most to apply to. Close this time by reading Ephesians 3:20–21.

talking SHOCK

Outline of a talk

The Bible talks very practically and realistically about drugs – because of the time at which it was written, the main drug it talks about is alcohol. Parts of the Bible commend the sensible use of drugs, both medicinally (1 Timothy 5:23) and for recreation (Psalm 104:14–15). Right at the beginning of the Bible is the story of Noah, who is well known for receiving a blessing after surviving the flood, but less well known for being the cause of a curse after getting drunk and stripping off (Genesis 9:20–21). It is the first of many warnings that drugs can make good people act uncharacteristically foolishly or destructively (Proverbs 20:1).

Jesus seemed to accept drinking, eating, and going to parties as part of life's joy – so much so that he was accused of being a glutton. His first recorded miracle was to turn water into wine at a wedding reception where the drink was running out (John 2:3–10). It was a great blessing, but also a symbol of the richness of the kingdom he was establishing, so radically new and exhilarating that he compared it to new wine (Matthew 9:17).

What the Bible doesn't do is give strict guidelines on how much it is right for people to drink (or use other drugs). And adults give out confusing signals – even Christian adults! Very few abstain completely from all drugs (especially not tea and coffee – the caffeine in these is both addictive and a stimulant, and can lead to athletes being banned for overuse).

Some Christians abstain from alcohol, while others are more liberal. Some smoke tobacco while others don't. There are a few, but not many, who support the legalisation of cannabis because there are arguments that, being practically non-addictive, it is the best way to control the alarming damage that more dangerous drugs are doing. This all sends out very confusing signals. When adults say, 'We don't want young people to do drugs,' but use drugs themselves, it isn't clear what they mean.

The most important thing you can do is to make wise decisions, and to know why you have made them. And the most useful thing in ensuring your decisions are wise is to be well educated about what each drug does to you, both bad and good, both body and mind. These decisions have to be reached in an atmosphere where it is possible to think straight without drugs in front of you, since it is extremely difficult to reach a godly decision during a party!

What we are all looking for is true freedom. And that is what Jesus promised his followers (John 8:31–36). Total permission to do anything at all is not freedom. Doing something risky because other people you know do it is not freedom. Falling for advertising is not freedom. Doing something because you are addicted and can't take the pain of not doing it is certainly not freedom. True freedom is coming to a godly decision despite the pressures that say 'Anything goes'. Paul pleaded with

Christians not be squeezed into the mould the world wants to get them in, but to be transformed by thinking in a completely new way (Romans 12:2).

Some things to remember

- God thinks your physical body is important, so nothing that damages it is a good idea (1 Corinthians 6:19–20). This includes eating fatty foods, avoiding exercise, sunbathing without protection and breathing car fumes, even though Christian adults don't get as excited about these as they do about drugs.
- Part of freedom is not just deciding for yourself, but wanting good things for others as well – so, for example, you need to be aware of what your smoke does to other people's lungs (Galatians 5:13–15).
- The decision should be made between you individually and God – so don't let your mind be made up by those who have got a vested interest in persuading you to do something you are not happy about.

Some stories, facts and quotations to help you

- *After years of research and development, scientists are at last able to announce that they have invented a device which can infallibly detect even the minutest quantity of any kind of drug in the air about a person. It's called a parent.*

- *And yet they drink, they laugh;*
Close the wound, hide the scar…
Carly Simon

- *First the man takes a drink, then the drink takes a drink, then the drink takes the man.*
Japanese proverb

- *Charlie Sheen was a bloated boozer until he dropped in backstage at a U2 concert in Phoenix, Arizona. Fresh from Platoon and Wall Street, Oliver Stone's parables of good and bad daddies duelling for the souls of impressionable youths, the bratpack star lurched into U2's dressing room waving a bottle of Jack Daniels and asked Bono how the band managed to do what they did. 'For a start, we don't do that,' retorted Bono, pointing at Sheen's bottle. Next day, Sheen embarked on a new regime of abstinence and exercise.*
The Observer, 23 October 1988

- *Wine is a mocker and beer a brawler;*
whoever is led astray by them is not wise.
Proverbs 20:1

Smoking – the bad news:

- *Of every 1000 young people who smoke, one will be murdered, six will die in road accidents, 250 will die prematurely as a result of smoking.*
- *The average smoker shortens his or her life by five years.*
- *Babies born to women who smoke weigh, on average, half a pound less than babies born to non-smokers.*

Smoking – the good news:

- *There are now ten million ex-smokers in Britain.*
- *The percentage of smokers is falling in every group in society, except girls in their teens.*
- *Seven out of ten smokers now say they want to give up.*

Reasons young people give for smoking (AGB Survey):

- *Friends, social reasons, relaxation ... 84%*
- *Calmness, soothing nerves, stops worry ... 61%*
- *Stops boredom ... 11%*
- *Enjoy the taste ... 11%*
- *Helps me diet ... 9%*
- *Helps me know what to do with my hands ... 5%*
- *Like the shape or glow ... 3%*
- *It's good for you ... 3%*

- *Those most affected by legalisation (of soft drugs) would be young people, many of whom do not use drugs because the habit is illegal. They would be able to say, 'If the state has okayed it, it can't be that bad!' and they would try, and get hooked.*
But drugs will continue to be sold as long as people are prepared to pay for them, the trade has an estimated value of over £5 billion a year in the UK alone. In the long run, the fight will only be won when people are properly informed of the dangers drugs pose.
The Guardian, 20 April 1994

- *Young people are naturally curious. Many are searching for an experience that transcends the crass materialism that they see in their culture. This and the affluence ... of young people have given the various elements of organised crime a strong incentive to exploit this rapidly expanding population. There is an amazingly effective worldwide operation for the manufacture and marketing of drugs at huge profits.*
Professor Jay E Adams

- *Cocaine is God's way of telling you you've got too much money.*
Robin Williams (actor)

What E can do for you (ecstasy, tabs):

- *Speed up the action of the central nervous system.*
- *Alter perception to give artificial feeling of well-being.*
- *Heighten reality, colours and sounds.*
- *Allow you to go on dancing for a very long time.*

What E can also do for you:

- *Cause hallucinations, confusion, subsequent depression.*
- *Cause heart problems.*
- *Cause traumatic dehydration through over-exertion (to which clubs contribute by turning off tap-water in the toilets, so that young people have to buy expensive drinks at the bar).*
- *Lead you to drink dangerously excessive amounts of water to over compensate.*
- *Cause loss of judgment and self-control.*
- *Cause psychological dependence.*
- *Cause panic.*
- *And inadequately prepared batches from untrustworthy suppliers kill people.*

afterSHOCK

- Kaleidoscope Project, 40 Cromwell Road, Kingston-upon-Thames, Surrey, KT2 6RE; telephone 0181-549 2681.
- The Institute for the Study of Drug Dependence, Waterbridge House, 32-36 Loman Street, London SE1 0EE; telephone 0171-928 1211.
- The Advisory Council on Alcohol and Drug Education, 1 Hulme Place, The Crescent, Salford, Manchester, M5 4QA; telephone 0161-745 8925.
- Re-Solve (Society for the Prevention of Solvent and Volatile Substance Abuse), 30a High Street, Stone, Staffordshire, ST15 8AW; telephone (01785) 817885.
- Hope UK, 25f Copperfield Street, London, SE1 0EN.
- Yeldall Christian Centres, Yeldall Manor, Hare Hatch, Reading, RG10 9XR; telephone (01734) 404411.

8 Issues concerned with... appearance and fashion

PART 1

SHOCK drama

A Grim Fairy Tale

CHARACTERS

- **Narrator**
- **Prime Minister** (male)
- **Michael**
- **Two extras who play all the other parts** (image consultants, journalists, royalty, celebrities, children)

PROPS

A screen

A change of clothes

Narrator: Once upon a time, in a land not so very far away, lived a Prime Minister. He enjoyed doing his job, and governed the land to the best of his ability. Well, no one's perfect! *(Enter the PM.)* One day the Prime Minister was day-dreaming and looking out of his office window.

The PM: I beg your pardon!

Narrator: What? Oh, I'm sorry! I mean, one day the Prime Minister was reflecting creatively on the state of the nation and examining the external inter-governmental outlook.

The PM: That's better!

Narrator: His trusted adviser, Michael, burst into the room.

Michael: Good morning, Prime ... Oh sir, what are we wearing today? Our suit doesn't suit us one bit. And that tie is not our colour at all!

Narrator: Now, Michael had been known in the past to tell the truth – which isn't suitable behaviour for a member of parliament at all. But the Prime Minister still trusted him. What he didn't know was that Michael was secretly after the Prime Minister's job, and this was just the beginning of a plot to undo him. Which is why he said...

The PM: Do you really think so, Michael?

Michael: Well sir, to be brutally honest, we haven't been looking ourselves at all recently. Our hair needs a bit of a cut, our suits are not quite what we want for television, and our glasses are just a little bit old fashioned. Everybody knows that nowadays what we look like is far more important than our policies. With the party conference coming up next month, now is the time to act.

The PM: So what are you suggesting?

Michael: Only one thing will do, sir. A change of image!

Narrator: So, even though the Prime Minister felt quite happy with the way he looked, the image consultants were called in.
(Enter the extras as image consultants. They mime measuring, manicuring, brushing the PM.)

Narrator: They fussed and fiddled round the Prime Minister for days on end. They measured everything there was to be measured. They combed and cut; they moisturised and manicured. They held up endless pieces of fabric and said:

1: Ooh, what a lovely shade.

Narrator: And...

2: Oh no, too bourgeois.
(A screen is drawn in front of the PM, who disappears behind it with the image consultants. During the next speech there is a great deal of activity behind the screen. Jackets and shirts get tossed in the air. Squeals and groans emerge.)

Narrator: And so they went into private session. And an expectant press corps waited. Weeks went by and the party conference season came round. Even the public were more excited than they usually get about politics, because the tabloids had been full of headlines about the Prime Minister's new image. It was undoubtedly the most important political development of the decade. There were leaks and there were lobbies, there were profiles and there were predications. And finally the day came for the Prime Minister to show his new image to the party faithful and the waiting millions.

The PM: *(From behind the screen.)* I'm really not sure at all about this.

Michael: *(Trying unsuccessfully to peep behind the screen.)* It will be splendid, sir. We all know it will. We've paid a vast amount of money for this, so how could it possibly not be splendid?

The PM: But I ... but I ...

Michael: No buts, sir! The world's press is here!
(The extras reappear as journalists.)

Michael: Everyone will think how trendy we are, sir. Now is the moment!
(The screen is pulled away. The PM is wearing a miniature bow tie, Mickey Mouse boxer shorts, red socks, and nothing else.)

The PM: Well, what do you think?

Michael: It's ... it's ...

1: How much did it cost?

The PM: Ten thousand pounds.

2: Ten grand! Magnificent! There's no doubt about it.

1: Sensational. A completely new concept in British politics.

2: A triumph of money over matter.

1: The voters will reward you with a landslide.

2: Stop the press. This is a scoop.
(They dash off.)

The PM: But, Michael, won't it be a bit perky in Parliament; a bit chilly in the chamber?

Michael: Sir! Sir! Think of the opinion polls. Think of the by-elections! ... Think of the money we've spent!

Narrator: And before long, the compliments were flowing in, from the highest in the land...
(One of the extras appears as royalty.)

1: One will be wearing the same to the state opening of Parliament. *(Exit.)*

Narrator: ... To the lowest forms of life.
(The other extra appears as some recognisable icon of contemporary culture, such as Mr Blobby.)

2: Blobby blobby blobby.
(Or similar celebrity catchphrase. Exit.)

Michael: They love us, sir. Our popularity rating is at an all-time high. People describe us as statesmanlike, noble, wise. Now is the time to call an election. We'll demolish the Opposition. Make them unelectable!

Narrator: And that is just what the Prime Minister did. He called an election the very next day. The opinion polls went soaring. The Opposition gave up bothering. The economy expanded unprecedentedly. And, on the eve of the election, the Prime Minister held the biggest political rally of all time. A youth rally, because he knew that was where the future of the country lay!
(The extras appear, on their knees, as flag-waving children.)

Narrator: And, confident of victory, he stood up to speak...

The PM: Boys and girls, tomorrow your Mummies and Daddies are going to elect me as...

1: Daddy, why's that funny man got no clothes on?

Michael: Shh! Listen to the Prime Minister.

2: He has. He's got no clothes on. Hee hee hee!

Michael: Behave yourselves. That image cost a lot of money.

1: He's in the nude! He's in the nude!
(Their laughter increases.)

Michael: Get this brat out of here.

2: He's got hairy legs! *(More laughter – even from the narrator.)*

Michael: I'm warning you. *(But he can't help laughing either.)*

1: He's got a wobbly tummy! *(Hilarity.)*

2: And a tiny, tiny, tiny little bow tie! *(Michael and the extras on the floor, laughing. The Prime Minister recoils in shock, covers up his torso as best he can, and sinks to the ground.)*

Narrator: Suddenly the Prime Minister realised how silly he had been. And the whole country realised how silly they had been. But they still went out and voted for him the next day, because up and down the land they had copied his example and they were too proud to admit that they had been duped. And what happened to them all? Well, the Prime Minister took advantage of the nationwide cover-up to introduce a clothing tax. He realised that Michael's idea had been a nasty plot all along, and he punished him by promoting him to Minister for Education. And what of the little boy who was so intelligent, clear-sighted and brilliant in every way imaginable? Well, he grew up to be a narrator of drama sketches. And wherever he went, his work was greeted with tumultuous rounds of applause...

short sharp SHOCK

To be announced to the whole group as a dilemma

The Bod-U-Like Surgery spent 2008 developing a surgical technique that is effective mostly on teenagers to change their physical appearance cheaply and safely. The most common operations for girls are to make them slimmer, and for boys, to increase penis size. There are also operations to reverse balding, change chest size, and alter skin colour. The increase in beautiful-looking teenagers is dramatic. The process has become hugely popular. For genetic reasons which are not yet clear, brown-eyed people cannot have the operations because a fatal internal reaction takes place. Brown-eyed people have come to be seen as significantly less attractive, and the result has been an alarming rise in depression, eating disorders and suicides among the 'browns'! The government is very concerned. It has two choices – to ban all operations which 'improve' appearance (which would be extremely unpopular and lose tax income), or to invest research money in extending the operations safely to brown-eyed people.

For discussion in small groups:

Which should they do?

ART 2

bible SHOCK

For discussion in small groups

❶ 1 Read Psalm 139:1–18. Pray that this discussion will lead to everyone feeling more at peace about the way God has made them, and developing the right kind of pride in the way they present themselves.

❷ Read verses 13–14 again. If it is true that God perfectly creates every human to be born with a particular appearance, shape and size, he must find everyone he creates beautiful. So why do humans find some people ugly and some beautiful?

❸ Read verses 15–16 again. Should we deduce from this that it is wrong to try to change the appearance God has given us? Make a list of the ways that people try to change their appearance (start with getting a sun tan, wearing make-up, having silicon implants – keep going until there is a list of a dozen or more). For each item, decide whether this is an acceptable way of maximising God's gifts of appearance, or defying God's intention that we should be content with what he has given us. Now try to work out whether you can back up your decisions biblically or whether they are just personal taste – or is there no difference?

❹ Read 1 Samuel 16:1–13. Look again at verse 7. How important is physical attractiveness in choosing: (a) a boyfriend or girlfriend, (b) national and political leaders, (c) a friend? When does backing away from someone because of their appearance become prejudice?

❺ Read Ezekiel 16:8–14. It is a picture of how God intended his special people to be – confident, at ease with their physicality, dressed to their best advantage, and utterly dedicated to God. Of course, this is a metaphor, but what does it tell us about how God wants us to see ourselves? Now read verse 15. Is there a clue here about how to get our physical appearance in correct proportion to the rest of our lives?

SHOCK waves

Materials: Paper, pens.

Working in small groups, choose one of the anxieties to do with fashion and appearance which emerged during the Bible study as something that young people worry about. Write a letter as if to the agony aunt of a favourite magazine. Try to include some of the ideas that have emerged during the discussion. There are some ground rules – no identifiable person should be named or referred to in the letter, and the tone of it should be sympathetic rather than mocking.

PART 3

SHOCK absorber

Prayers and acts of praise in seven contrasting styles from which to choose

A selection of songs and hymns:

- It's Your blood, *Songs of Fellowship* (4)
- I'm accepted, *Songs of Fellowship* (4)
- I will change your name, *Songs of Fellowship* (4)
- In my life, Lord, *Songs of Fellowship* (2), *Mission Praise* (1)
- Let the beauty of Jesus, *Mission Praise* (1)
- O Lord, your tenderness, *Songs of Fellowship* (4), *Mission Praise* (2)
- Show me, dear Lord, *Songs of Fellowship* (5)
- When I look into Your holiness, *Songs of Fellowship* (3), *Mission Praise* (2)
- You laid aside Your majesty, *Songs of Fellowship* (3), *Mission Praise* (2)

Using the Shock Waves responses

Display the 'letters to an agony aunt' around the wall. Give everyone a chance to read them. Ask those present to work in small groups again. This time, they are to imagine that each letter has been intercepted by God on its way to the agony aunt. Choosing one of the letters on display, they should compose the letter God might send in reply which deals with the worry (the same ground rules apply). When this is completed, they should, as an act of worship, attach the reply to the wall underneath the letter it refers to. Allow time for them to look at each others' letters too and ask themselves what God might be saying to the group through it all.

Led prayer

Grant us, good Lord,
not to be anxious about earthly things,
but to love things heavenly;
and even now,
while we are placed among things that are passing away,
to hold fast to those things that shall endure,
through Jesus Christ our Lord,
who lives and reigns with you and the Holy Spirit,
one God, for ever and ever. Amen.

Book of Common Prayer (adapted)

Responsive prayer

These hands were made in the image of God,
These hands are precious to you.

These feet were made in the image of God,
These feet are precious to you.

These faces were made in the image of God,
These faces are precious to you.

These bodies were made in the image of God,
These bodies are precious to you.

These minds were made in the image of God,
These minds are precious to you.

These people were made in the image of God,
These people are precious to you.

These lives were made in the image of God,
These lives are precious to you. Amen.

Open prayer

Invite the group to divide into threes or fours and give each of them a teenage-targeted magazine. Ask them to flick through the magazine, especially the agony aunt page. In their groups, they should pray about issues which come to mind as they look through the magazine. Pray individually for the needs of the people who have written to the agony aunt, for the problems highlighted by the feature articles, for the fashion industry which shapes our views on appearance, for magazine editors and journalists, and for other issues which are known to worry their friends.

Silent reflection

During the course of the previous fortnight, collect images to show on screen in an audio-visual sequence. This could be done by:

***a** borrowing slides of people of all shapes, sizes, ages and colours from a keen photographer,*
***b** taking slides from a selection of colour magazines – you need an SLR camera, a close-up lens attachment, a fast film (ASA 200 or 400), and a table in front of a sunny window,*
***c** photocopying black and white overhead projector acetates from newspapers and magazines – you need an ordinary photocopier, but special, coarse photocopier acetates.*

Play a piece of music such as 'All I ever have to be', Amy Grant, from the album Never Alone, 'The busy girl needs beauty', Billy Bragg, Back to Basics, or 'Beautiful girl', INXS, Welcome to Wherever You Are and The Greatest Hits. As you do so, show the slides, for ten seconds at a time. As the music fades away, allow a time of silence. Begin it with the words of Genesis 1:26–27, 31:

God said, 'And now we will make human beings: they will be like us and resemble us' ... So God created human beings, making them to be like himself. He created them male and female, and he blessed them ... And God looked at what he had made, and he was very pleased.

Close the silence with this prayer by Reinhold Niebuhr:

O God, give us grace to accept with serenity the things that cannot be changed, the courage to change the things that should be changed, and the wisdom to distinguish the one from the other. Amen.

Creative prayer

Give each person a piece of A4 paper in a variety of colours and a pen. Ask them to fold the paper in half to give a long, thin shape. They should then tear out the shape of a human (tearing the vertical half of the figure out of the folded edge, so that it is symmetrical when the paper is opened). On the paper they should then draw (or write) in an appropriate place:

a something about their appearance that they like,
b something about themselves that they do not like,
c an attitude or feeling that they would like to change.

When this is done, they are to fold their shapes in half again so that no one else can see what they have done. The leader should say a prayer thanking God that he has created us in such a way that he thinks every type of appearance to be beautiful, and asking for his help so that we may increasingly see and accept ourselves the way God sees and accepts us. The 'torn people' should then be placed symbolically at the foot of a cross. As the group stands round the cross, say together the words from 2 Corinthians 13:13.

talking SHOCK

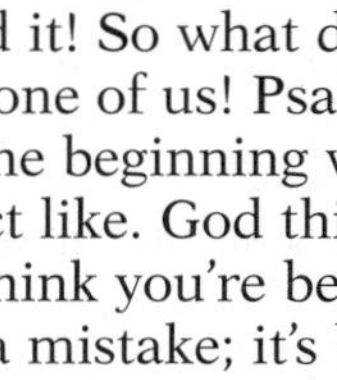

Outline of a talk

Every one of us is affected by the world's biggest marketing ploy – the perfect body. Because of it, people who have never seen us succeed in persuading us that we want to be taller, shorter, thinner, fatter, prettier, have a different hair colour, or just have hair. But what *is* the perfect body? In the 50s it was the hour-glass figure for women, in the 60s it was waif-like thinness. In the 90s the perfect body is well-toned and muscular from constant exercise. The irony is that we listen to advertising experts, who sell us the latest trend, instead of medical experts, who tell us that each person's body has a weight and shape that it likes to be. Ever wondered why clothes look out of date so quickly? Because someone is making lots of money out of that!

Is God anti-beauty? Certainly not. One of the books in the Bible rejoices in celebrating physical beauty (Song of Songs 4:1–7 – full of comic potential when read today, but seriously erotic one thousand years before Jesus). God knows all about beauty. He created it! So what does he think is beautiful? Every single one of us! Psalm 139:13–16 tells us he knew from the beginning what we would look like, be like, act like. God thinks you are beautiful. If you don't think you're beautiful, it's not because God made a mistake; it's because the people who make you think badly of yourself are making a mistake.

Is the way we look relevant to the way God wants us to live? Jesus told us not to distress ourselves with worry over what we look like – particularly over the size of various bits of us (Matthew 6:25–27). God will look after our needs in these areas, because he understands them – if he can make nature so beautiful, you are no problem (Matthew 6:30–32)!

If God wants us to be happy with the way we are, it doesn't mean that it is wrong to want to dress well, to do exercise, or to achieve a healthy weight. That is all part of being a confident person who enjoys being himself or herself. But it does mean working out where to draw the line between self-acceptance and vanity!

Three pieces of advice:

- Be aware that we are all being manipulated by fashion. We will never 'arrive' in fashion because it will always change. But there are some valuable things about you which don't change. Next time you are about to blow your life's savings on a pair of trainers, stop a minute to ask yourself who persuaded you that you need them. Making your own decision is freedom – the kind of freedom Jesus said his followers would find (John 8:36).

- See the best in other people. Cut the derogatory comments. Positively and honestly help your mates choose clothes that suit them. It is all part of encouraging one another and having each others' best interests at heart (Philippians 2:1–4).

- Think about what you are portraying to people through what you wear. Let it be a decision that reflects the best in you, not a bad accident! Somewhere between fashion-martyr and anorak-wearer there is a way of looking good and being at ease with yourself without being trapped by the fashion industry. A whole generation of Christians who feel able to do that would have a great impact for good on the world around them.

Some stories, facts and quotations to help you

- *My one regret in life is that I am not someone else.*
Woody Allen

- *What I am in God's sight is what I am. No more; no less.*
St Francis of Assisi

- *Schwarzenegger is my idol, and whether God intended me to be like him or not, that is what I have always wanted.*
Robert, 27 (interviewed in Cosmopolitan magazine, after spending £8,000 to have silicon implants in his chest and legs)

- *Your brain is the most complex structure known to man. Your eyes can distinguish up to one million colour surfaces. Your lungs are big enough to cover half a tennis court. You have around 60 thousand miles of blood vessels. Your skin is constantly replacing itself. You give birth to 100 billion red blood cells every day. Your bones are as strong as cast iron. Your heart beats 100 thousand times a day. You're amazing. We want you to stay that way.*
BUPA medical insurance advertisement

- *When I became a Christian and I had all my hair dyed green and orange and that, I says to myself, it's not going to be very nice if people say to me, 'Are you a Christian?' and I'm standing there with rips in my clothes, safety pins all over, and my hair dyed, 'cos they'll say, 'If that's a Christian, I don't want anything to do with that.' So I changed.*
Barry (Teenage Beliefs, David Day and Philip May)

- *By the age of sixteen, more than 50% of women are dissatisfied with their bodies.*
Statistics from Cleo magazine.

- *I hate my body; I hate my hair, my eyes, my looks. I don't like myself at all. And as for the voice; they all go on about the voice. I don't know what the hell it is. Ask me again when I'm in the grave.*
Richard Burton (arguably the greatest actor of his day)

- *I'm looking at the man in the mirror,*
I'm asking him to make the change.
No message could appear any clearer...
If you want to make the world a better place
Take a look at yourself and make the change.
Michael Jackson

Some facts and figures about cosmetic surgery:

- *The first face-lift was performed in Paris in 1906.*
- *The major impetus toward the development of reconstructive surgical techniques was the horrific injuries suffered by soldiers during World War of 1914-1918.*
- *In London in 1816, two patients were successfully operated on to restore their noses. The first purely cosmetic nose surgery was performed in 1840.*
- *There are now over 130 clinics operating in the UK, treating an estimated 50-60 thousand patients every year. 80% of patients are women.*